T0194093

NUGGETS OF GOLD

FROM THE ASH PIT

Michael Howard

WESTBOW
PRESS®
A DIVISION OF THOMAS NELSON
& ZONDERVAN

Scripture quotations taken from the New American Standard Bible® (NASB), Copyright © 1960, 1962, 1963, 1968, 1971, 1972, 1973, 1975, 1977, 1995 by The Lockman Foundation. Used by permission. www.Lockman.org

Scripture quotations marked (KJV) taken from the King James Version of the Bible.

Scripture quotations marked (NIV) are taken from the Holy Bible, New

International Version®, NIV®. Copyright © 1973, 1978, 1984, 2011 by Biblica, Inc.™ Used by permission of Zondervan. All rights reserved worldwide. www. zondervan.com The "NIV" and "New International Version" are trademarks registered in the United States Patent and Trademark Office by Biblica, Inc.™

Scripture taken from the New King James Version®. Copyright © 1982 by Thomas Nelson. Used by permission. All rights reserved.

Scripture quotations marked MSG are taken from THE MESSAGE, copyright © 1993, 1994, 1995, 1996, 2000, 2001, 2002 by Eugene H. Peterson. Used by permission of NavPress. All rights reserved. Represented by Tyndale House Publishers, Inc

Scripture quotations marked (NLT) are taken from the Holy Bible, New Living Translation, copyright ©1996, 2004, 2007, 2013, 2015 by Tyndale House Foundation. Used by permission of Tyndale House Publishers, Inc., Carol Stream, Illinois 60188. All rights reserved

Scriptures marked NASU are taken from the NEW AMERICAN STANDARD UPDATED (NASU): Scripture taken from the NEW AMERICAN STANDARD UPDATED BIBLE®, copyright©, 1995 by The Lockman Foundation. Used by permission

WestBow Press books may be ordered through booksellers or by contacting:

WestBow Press
A Division of Thomas Nelson & Zondervan
1663 Liberty Drive
Bloomington, IN 47403
www.westbowpress.com
1 (866) 928-1240

ISBN: 978-1-9736-1805-8 (sc)
ISBN: 978-1-9736-1804-1 (hc)
ISBN: 978-1-9736-1806-5 (e)

Library of Congress Control Number: 2018901377

Print information available on the last page.

WestBow Press rev. date: 02/22/2018

This book is dedicated to Elizabeth Ray, whose tireless efforts and boundless enthusiasm for the English language were instrumental in assuring that I gained the ability to write a complete, coherent sentence.

ACKNOWLEDGMENTS

This book would not have come into being without the contributions of many other people. Chief among these is my wife, Joy, who has supported me throughout our marriage no matter what crackpot schemes I devise. Her support and encouragement are the foundation of everything I accomplish. Thank you for being the better part of me.

Next comes my mother, Mae, and Joy's mother, Mary, whom I referred to as my "other mother." These women always suspected that I had more in me than just building bridges. You both believed in me.

Finally, I would like to thank all the friends who read my writings and encouraged me to continue on this path. Your willingness to read my unfinished work and share your thoughts and suggestions should not go unnoticed. My gratitude to all of you.

PROLOGUE

The mines had played out years ago. There were no miners left. The equipment lay abandoned, rusting and rotting away, not worth the trouble of saving. The mines were simply empty holes once filled with hopes and dreams, now abandoned to vermin and scavengers.

Near the holes were the tailings, the leftover rubble from the mining operations. There were great piles of these tailings, which were by far the largest percentage of what the mines had produced. For every ounce of gold the mines had found, there were hundreds of pounds of tailings. They were heaped up outside the entrances to the mines. The wilderness was reclaiming them a little at a time, beginning first with grasses and vines and finally with small trees growing in the rejected rubble of the mining refuse.

To this scene comes the old prospector. His back is bent. His hat is slouched and his clothes are worn. His donkey is tired. They both move slowly and carefully, picking their way through the rubble to a place where hope exists. Sometimes these tailing piles contain bits of gold that were missed. It is not a lucrative way to make a living, but it is safer than trying to work the abandoned mines.

The prospector slowly lifts his pick and begins to dig. The pick makes a metallic clink as it strikes the rocks of the pile of refuse. Hour after hour, he pecks away at the heap of debris. Sweat drips off his brow and soaks his shirt. He stops and looks at what he has dug, grasping at hope. Hope is the reason he is here. Hope drives him forward. Finally, there is a glint of something in the dust: a nugget overlooked by the original miners, a treasure in an abandoned pile of waste, shines brightly. It is huge, larger than any expectation the old prospector had. A nugget this size could sustain him for many years to come.

He stares in disbelief and examines it closely. He has seen fool's gold before, the deceptively shiny iron pyrite. This is not fool's gold—it's gold! This is the real deal. He stands up, nugget in hand. His back is no longer bent. He has new energy. Even the tired donkey seems to be endowed with new vitality. The prospector lets out a jubilant whoop and dances a little jig in celebration. Hope has turned to reality.

*

For many Christians,* the book of Job is like the tailings pile of the mine of scripture. It is filled with the things we do not like: death, destruction, suffering, and loss. It is grown over

---

* If you have been given this book or have just picked it up, and you are not a Christian, please see the Appendix near the end of this book. If you are not yet a Christian, do not give up here. Although the ideas and principles in this book are written mainly with Christians in mind, even a nonbeliever may benefit from this book, but much greater benefits await those who trust in Christ.

with the accusations of would-be friends, and it's inhabited by the scavengers and vermin of bitterness. It conjures up an image of an old man, broken and abandoned, sitting in an ash pit or a refuse pile of a Middle Eastern city, scraping his sores with broken bits of pottery. No, we do not like the book of Job. Still, it is in there. It is still part of God's message to us. It is inescapable. It beckons to us to understand the mystery.

To borrow a line from Meredith Wilson's *Music Man*, the book of Job is full of "Trouble with a capital T," but so is life. We have trouble in this life—maybe not every day, all day long, but it is inevitable. We all have troubles in our lives, and ours seem to be the ones with a capital T. River City had a pool hall. Some of us have financial woes, a chronic illness, family disputes, religious persecution, fears, worries and depression, or any number of other troubles. The one thing we have in common is that we all have trouble. From the greatest to the least, everyone has some trouble in his life. Maybe it's not to the extreme level of Job, but trouble is waiting for each of us. How do we deal with this inescapable trouble? Maybe we can find the answers in a book that seems to be filled with trouble.

This is where I found myself many years ago. Trouble was overwhelming me defeat after defeat, loss upon loss. I was ruined. Therefore I searched for answers in the book of Trouble. "If Job came through this, then maybe I could do things the way he did," I reasoned. I read the book and then read it again. I didn't get it. I wasn't seeing the point. It was just words on a page. I was looking for a magical solution to all my troubles, an escape hatch.

I was young and didn't know any better. I didn't understand then what I know now. Sometimes we simply have to keep on going, to continue doing what is right even though things don't seem to be getting better. I wish I'd had a guide through all the troubles of that time.

Recently there was a news story about a veterinarian who took off his wedding ring while performing surgery on one of his patients. He set it carefully aside, but somehow when the trash from the surgery was gathered up, the ring was in with the trash. By the time he realized the ring was missing, the trash truck had already emptied the clinic's dumpster. The veterinarian was devastated, but he didn't give up hope. He and his wife raced to the landfill where the trash truck had gone. They asked the man in charge of the dump where the truck would have dumped their trash. The man directed them to the place, and they began to dig through the nasty pile of garbage. By persistence, they found the ring and were able to rejoice and share their good fortune with others through the news.

The part of this story that jumped out at me was that the couple asked for help from the one person who was able to help them: the expert, the one with knowledge of the trash dump. The supervisor was able to guide them to the right place and make the search go faster. They might have eventually found the ring without his help, but asking him made the search go faster. They had a guide to make the search faster. It was still a lot of garbage to sort through, but they knew they were on the right track because their guide had directed them.

I had a guide too. I simply didn't recognize him at the time.

There were probably others, godly men and women surrounding me whom I was ignoring because they weren't telling me what I wanted to hear. I was looking for a way out instead of the way to press through.

I had a guide in the Holy Spirit, who was gently guiding me through His other scriptures in the way that I should walk. It was only later, after walking out those scriptures for years and experiencing the wonderful peace, provision, and protection of my heavenly Father, that I was able to go back to the book of Job and find the nuggets of hope and encouragement.

The book of Job is a place where we do not often go, but it is a place where treasure awaits if we are willing to dig for it. There are nuggets of gold in the ash pit if we take the time to sort through the many words. It is a book that is filled with hope and promise of things to come, with comfort and encouragement for now, and with promise of redemption later. It is the tailings pile, the ash pit of scripture, but it contains nuggets of gold that can sustain us in good times, and it can give us hope and encouragement when we find ourselves in the ash pit of life. The book of Job contains golden nuggets of hope. I hope that I can be your guide and smooth the search for nuggets, but mostly I pray that the Spirit of God will guide you as we dig for gold in the ash pit.

How do we deal with trouble? Why must we deal with trouble? What is the source of our trouble, and where is our relief? Are we condemned to suffer, or are we able to overcome and persevere? I believe the answers to these questions and others can be found in the oldest book of the Bible, the book of Job.

Most Christians regard this book as the Big Downer of the

Bible because it is full of death and destruction, lamentation and accusation. When we think of Job, the image of an old man sitting alone in the ash heap, scraping his festering sores with a broken piece of pottery, comes to mind. It depresses us to even think about Job. Job was a man who had it all, and then he had it all taken away. But the Bible is not a book that is meant to depress us or bring us down. On the contrary, it is meant to lift us up into God's presence and bring us into communion with Him. We can readily see this in books like Paul's letter to the Romans and the Gospel of John. The encouragement fairly jumps off the page when we read, "We are more than conquerors," and, "God so loved the world." But, when it comes to Job, we have to dig a little deeper in the ash pit to find encouragement.

It is there, though, and we can find it.

NUGGET #1

God Is Good

Then the Lord said to Satan, "Behold, all that he has is in your power, only do not put forth your hand on him." So Satan departed from the presence of the Lord. (Job 1:12)

There are a lot of ashes in the book of Job. Most of the book takes place in the ash pit as Job mourns his losses. Job underwent a test that most of us doubt we could endure. This scares us because we know that God is no respecter of persons. If He chose to test Job, He could choose to test us too. We don't like to think about ourselves or our families going through a time of testing like Job's. But the test is not the point of what this book is teaching us. It is how the test accomplishes its purpose that is important. We will deal with that in more detail as we sift through the ashes. But suffice it to say, there are lessons to be learned, encouragement to be received, and blessings of God to increase in our lives. Are you excited yet? Probably not, but I certainly hope you will be before we are done. Let's start digging and see what turns up. Our first nugget comes to us through the ash pit, but its source is the very throne room of heaven.

> Then the Lord said to Satan, "Behold, all that
> he has is in your power, only do not put forth
> your hand on him." So Satan departed from the
> presence of the Lord. (Job 1:12)

This is the true gem of the book of Job, if we look at it correctly. We often do not. We see God as taking some sort of perverse joy in Job's suffering, or using him as a pawn in some sort of chess game of one-upmanship with Satan. This is far from the truth, however. There is a contest going on, but Job is not a pawn. A pawn is a piece of very low value and strategic power, which a player will often sacrifice in order to capture a more valuable piece. Job is not valueless or weak. Neither is he simply a piece being moved about against his will on the chessboard of life. He has free will and is able to exercise it as he sees fit. He may not have chosen the circumstances in which he found himself, but he is free to react to them as he wishes. He is not a valueless piece to be sacrificed for a greater goal. Look at how God speaks about him. God is practically bragging about Job's upright character.

> The Lord said to Satan, "Have you considered My
> servant Job? For there is no one like him on the
> earth, a blameless and upright man, fearing God
> and turning away from evil." (Job 1:8)

This is not the way one speaks of a pawn that is sacrificed at will. This is the way one speaks of a beloved son who just made a tackle on the football field, or of a daughter who sang a solo and wowed the crowd. He is looking at His child and admiring his character, saying, "My child has turned out quite well." God is not simply using Job to show up Satan. He is a proud papa bragging about His child. He is proud of Job's accomplishments, but more than that, He is proud of Job's uprightness. Righteousness is Job's main character trait. But evil is just around the corner.

This chapter deals with the age-old problem, "Why is there evil in the world?" The simple answer is that there is evil in the world because first there was evil in heaven. Lucifer was the most beautiful of all God's angels. The book of Ezekiel shows this in detail:

> You had the seal of perfection,
> Full of wisdom and perfect in beauty.
> You were in Eden, the garden of God;
> Every precious stone was your covering:
> The ruby, the topaz and the diamond;
> The beryl, the onyx and the jasper;
> The lapis lazuli, the turquoise and the emerald;
> And the gold, the workmanship of your settings and sockets,
> Was in you.
> On the day that you were created
> They were prepared.
> You were the anointed cherub who covers,
> And I placed you there.
> You were on the holy mountain of God;
> You walked in the midst of the stones of fire.
> You were blameless in your ways
> From the day you were created
> Until unrighteousness was found in you. (Ezek. 28:12–15)

This passage speaks of a lovely angel, beautiful in his own right and created to worship God in heaven. But then unrighteousness was found in him. Evil had shown itself. What was this evil? It was pride.

How you have fallen from heaven,
O star of the morning, son of the dawn!
You have been cut down to the earth,
You who have weakened the nations!
But you said in your heart,
"I will ascend to heaven;
I will raise my throne above the stars of God,
And I will sit on the mount of assembly
In the recesses of the north.
"I will ascend above the heights of the clouds;
I will make myself like the Most High."
Nevertheless you will be thrust down to Sheol,
To the recesses of the pit. (Isa. 14:12–15)

Lucifer rebelled against God and was cast out of heaven. (It seems he was able or maybe even required to show himself before God from time to time.) He was given a new name, Satan, which means the accuser. The New Testament Greek translated this word as *diabolos*, which the King James translators rendered as *devil*. But its more accurate meaning is false accuser. From this word we get our English word *diabolical*, which means atrociously evil, inhuman, or devilish. This is the source of evil in the world. We must remember that the book of Job calls him the accuser, but the New Testament makes it very clear that he is the *false* accuser.

If any piece of truth comes out of him, it is twisted to conform to his lying nature. He is the Father of Lies (John 8:44).

Into the presence of God comes this liar and false accuser. God, the omniscient one, asks him where he has been. Satan's answer is typically evasive. "Oh, here and there, there and here, you know." I'm paraphrasing here, but this is the gist of what Satan is saying. He's waiting for God to make the first move. (Job 1: 7)

God then begins boasting about His beloved servant. (Job 1: 8) He calls him blameless and upright—a man who fears God and shuns evil. This is praise from the one who is worthy of praise. To be commended by God as worthy of His praise is an awesome thing. Satan himself had received this commendation of God before he fell, and the fact that the praises are now Job's rankles him. Satan opens his mouth and begins to lie.

> Then Satan answered the Lord, "Does Job fear God for nothing? Have You not made a hedge about him and his house and all that he has, on every side? You have blessed the work of his hands, and his possessions have increased in the land. But put forth Your hand now and touch all that he has; he will surely curse You to Your face." (Job 1:9–11)

Part of this is true, which is typical of Satan's tactics. Lies are easier to swallow when washed down with a few half-truths. Yes, God had blessed Job greatly, but this was not the reason that Job served God. Job served God because serving God was the right thing. Job was not blameless because he was rich, and neither was he rich because he was blameless. His service to God was not because of his possessions. His service to God was because he feared God. We serve God not because He blesses us, and we do not receive blessing from God because we serve Him. We serve Him because He is worthy and deserving of our service. He blesses us because He is who He is—the God who blesses His children with all good things. Satan understands this but refuses to accept it. He tells God that if all Job's stuff is taken away, he will curse God instead of blessing Him. This is a lie, and God is ready to show it as such.

> Then the Lord said to *Satan*, "Behold, all that he has is in *your power*, only do not put forth your hand on him." So Satan departed from the presence of the Lord.
> (Job 1:12; my emphasis)

I emphasized these words in our first nugget from the ash pit to show what is really going on here. God has placed Job's stuff in Satan's power. The next time you read about Job's camels being driven off by the Chaldeans or the house collapsing on his children, remember this: *it is not God's doing.* Job's stuff was placed in Satan's hands. Satan didn't have to strike Job's possessions and family; he chose to strike them. God would have been perfectly content to let Job go on as he was. Satan is trying to make a point, but it fails because it is based on a lie. Job doesn't curse God. Instead, he blesses God.

> He said, "Naked I came from my mother's womb,
> And naked I shall return there.

The Lord gave and the Lord has taken away.
Blessed be the name of the Lord." (Job 1:21; my
emphasis)

If you take nothing away from this beside this one thing,
your life will still be blessed. God is *good*. This is the crux of the
matter. He did not want Job's stuff stricken. He was very happy
blessing His servant. The source of evil in this story is Satan. The
action of evil in this story is Satan's. Job is not stricken because
he sinned. Job is stricken because Satan struck him—period. The
ungodly look at the problem of evil and blame God, thinking He
is inactive at best or nonexistent at worst. A noted atheist writer
has written a book titled *God Is Not Great*. The writer's premise is
that if God exists at all, then because He allows evil in the world,
He is evil Himself.

We must recognize that God does not inflict evil upon the
world. He created both us and the angels with a free will. We
are free to serve or not serve Him. If He had done otherwise, we
would be nothing but automatons going through the motions. If
we have a free will to serve Him or not, then our service to Him
has meaning.

I can make a machine that will perform tasks for me. It will
bend to my will, and I can control its every move, but it will never
love me and serve me. It is simply a machine doing what it is doing.

We are not machines going through the motions. We are free
moral beings who serve or reject our creator as the result of our
own will. Satan, also a free moral agent, chose to strike Job's stuff,
and his scheme failed. Job made a choice to serve God.

We also have free will. We can serve God, or we can reject Him. This is the choice that He gave, and it was a costly choice for Him. It cost him the death of Jesus on the cross. When Adam sinned, it was by his free will. When we accept Jesus's sacrifice on the cross by our will, we overcome the evil with our faith in Jesus. The evil in the world was defeated at the cross. We are just walking out the rest of the victory over evil as we lead our lives in obedience to Christ.

> Then the Lord said to Satan, "Behold, all that he has is in your power, *only do not put forth your hand on him.*" So Satan departed from the presence of the Lord.
> (Job 1:12 my emphasis)

The second thing to consider is this. Even when God allowed the lying Satan to attack Job, He put limits on Satan's authority to do so. Satan was allowed to go this far and no more. God doesn't allow us to be tempted beyond that which we can bear.

> No temptation has overtaken you but such as is common to man; and God is faithful, who will not allow you to be tempted beyond what you are able, but with the temptation will provide the way of escape also, so that you will be able to endure it. (1 Cor. 10:13)

God places limits on our lives and limitations on how far Satan can go in his efforts to bring destruction. Sometimes by our own actions, we extend these limits, allowing Satan more reign in our lives by the choices we make. Understand that this is not God's best will for us, but He allows us to find our own way back from the far country of rebellion against Him. How does He do this? The answer is in the last half of the verse. He provides a way for escape—not to get us out of our trouble but to enable us to endure it or press on through to the end. The word that is translated *to escape* in the English Bible is *ekbasin*. This Greek word means to walk through or out of something. He doesn't immediately pull us out of our troubles. He enables us to walk through and out of them.

How do we apply this knowledge? Do we accept it on an intellectual basis and nothing more? In doing this, we say, "Yes God is good, but I still have trouble. So what?" Or do we thank God in advance for the good that is going to come from the trouble? This is hard to do, but it is the best way. It is often clearer and easier to deal with in retrospect. I'm sure Joseph had a hard time thanking God when his brothers threw him into a pit and sold him into slavery. But at the end, when he had a little perspective on the situation, he looked at things a little differently. These are Joseph's words to his brothers after the death and burial of their father.

> As for you, you meant evil against me, but God meant it for good in order to bring about this present result, to preserve many people alive. (Gen. 50:20–21)

When we suffer loss in this life, it is at the hands of the evil one. Whatever challenges he throws up in our way, he means for evil to harm us. God doesn't lie to us by calling evil good. He turns it around and brings something good from the ash pits of our lives. Notice that Joseph never justifies his brothers' actions. He says, "You meant evil against me." The evil that we suffer in this life is just that—evil. But God can use the evil that Satan intends for our harm, turning it around and using it to bring something good. Often we must wait until He has brought us through it to see the whole picture.

> And we know that God causes all things to work together for good to those who love God, to those who are called according to His purpose. (Rom. 8:28)

In the meantime, we should continue to walk through whatever comes our way, knowing that soon we will walk right out of the darkness and into a better understanding of God's plan for us.

For a minute, let's return to my story. During the economic recession of the 1980s, I was unemployed for a protracted period of time. Prospects for employment in my field of construction work were dim, and in late 1983 mine were nonexistent because I was also recovering from a softball injury that had left me on crutches. I was receiving unemployment benefits until I injured my ankle, which left me unable to work even if I had been able to find employment. When I injured my ankle, this left me without even the unemployment benefits. My wife and I were going through our savings to survive. This is the ash pit where I found myself.

I was angry, hurting, bitter, desperate, and looking for something to hold on to. This was when I first began to read the Bible in order to understand what it meant for me on a personal level. I read the book of Job, looking for answers, but it was just words on a page because I didn't see this fundamental truth of who the God of Abraham, Isaac, and Jacob is. I still imagined Him dealing out punishment to keep people toeing the line. I missed the whole point of the story. In my mind, He was punishing me for something I had done or not done. I didn't see that He was limiting the influence of evil until He could bring His plan to fruition.

He did have a plan for me. He had a plan for Job too, but first Job had to have more trouble and then a pity party.

NUGGET #2

The Crucible

But he said to her, "You speak as one of the foolish women speaks. Shall we indeed accept good from God and not accept adversity?" In all this Job did not sin with his lips. (Job 2:10)

Chapter 2 finds us again at the throne of God. Some time has passed, and once again Satan comes into the presence of God. It is interesting to note that God's testimony about Job has not changed. He still refers to Job in the same glowing terms with the added note, "although you [Satan] incited Me to ruin him without cause." God is pleased with the way Job has dealt with Satan's attacks, and He lets Satan know this.

Not to be outdone, Satan doubles down on his original bet.

> Satan answered the Lord and said, "Skin for skin! Yes, all that a man has he will give for his life. "However, put forth Your hand now, and touch his bone and his flesh; he will curse You to Your face." (Job 2:4–5)

Once again, God puts Job's fate in Satan's hand. It's not because He doesn't care, but more because He *does* care for Job. He wants to see Job triumph over adversity. He wants to see Satan's plans thwarted. The way to do this is to allow Job to experience adversity and triumph over it. Still, He puts limits on Satan's power to affect Job.

> "Behold, he is in your power, only spare his life."
> (Job 2:6)

This is where we find Job in chapter 2, sitting in the ashes and scraping his boils with a broken piece of pottery. His children are dead, his prosperity is stolen, and his health is failing. If Job were going to look at the bright side, he might say, "Well, at least I'm still alive. And I still have my wife." Oh, yeah—let's look at her.

This woman is a bit of an enigma. We don't know her name. We don't know any more about her than the two verses here tell us, except we can infer this one thing: she was hurting too. Her losses were as great as Job's. It was her children who died too. It was her prosperity that was lost. It was her position as the wife of a leader in the community that was taken when Job's fortunes were reversed. It was her husband whose health was failing as he sat in the ashes. Also, hurting people hurt people. Often it is the ones closest to them who are hurt the most. They lash out at whoever is handy. In this case, it was her husband, Job.

In her hurt and grief, she wanted it to be over. This seemed like a quick way out of the situation. Here was her husband, the pillar of the community, sitting in the ashes and blessing God. It was too much to take. She was angry at God, but Job was the one who was handy. When we are hurting, we often do the same thing.

> Then his wife said to him, "Do you still hold fast
> your integrity? Curse God and die!" (Job 2:9–10)

The way they both saw it, all Job had was his integrity, but they each had a little different perspective. Job said, "All my stuff is gone, but at least I still have my relationship with God." His wife said, "All our stuff is gone, and all we have is your relationship with God. What good has that done us?"

The Proverbs of Solomon tell us, "A soft answer turns away wrath."(Prov. 15:1 NKJV) I think with the situation being what it was, we'll give Job credit for as soft an answer as he could at the time.

> But he said to her, "You speak as one of the foolish
> women speaks. Shall we indeed accept good from
> God and not accept adversity?" (Job 2:10)

He didn't really call her foolish. He simply said she was speaking like one of the foolish women. This is not an indictment of all women, or even women in general. He did not say that all women are foolish. The Hebrew word here is *nabal*; it means stupid or foolish. Most often in the Old Testament, it refers to someone who is morally bankrupt or unbelieving.

> The fool hath said in his heart, There is no God.
> (Ps. 14:1 KJV)

Job told his wife that she was speaking like the ungodly unbelieving women who surrounded them. We too live in a land of unbelieving, foolish women and men. They reject God's ways and His Son. They revile His people and mock Him and them. They bring a curse on their lives, and most of them don't even recognize it.

The unbelievers would do just as she said: curse God and die. They would look at the adversity and say, "This is God's fault. He is tormenting me. I reject Him and all He represents." They might not die immediately as she seemed to suggest, but ultimately all the unbelievers will die—and when they do, their fate is far worse than any adversity that presents itself in this world.

For Job to do this would have been the same as physical death. Cursing God would have cut him off from his God. This is death to a believer. This was the integrity to which Job clung—his faith in God's goodness and his ultimate deliverance from sin and sickness and death.[1]

Job next poses a rhetorical question that again explores the same question of good and evil. "Shall we indeed accept good from God and not accept adversity?" If we consider the good things in our lives as gifts from God, then what do we make of the evil that comes to us? Is it also from God? Can the good and perfect God send us something that is evil? Job seems to assert this. If God can prosper us, He can also destroy us at His will. He destroyed the evildoers in Noah's day. He destroyed the Egyptians (although Job probably lived before that time, and so he makes no reference to this).[2]

The grammar of Job's sentence indicates that the source of the good is definitely God. It leaves in question somewhat the source of the evil. Some of the translations render the last word here as *evil* but I really like the NASB rendering of *adversity*. My own paraphrase of this verse would read, "Shall we expect to receive good things from the hand of God and then not expect that the enemy would oppose us by sending adversity and undesirable circumstances?" I know that I am taking a little liberty with the text here, but in the context of what is happening to Job, I think my assessment is accurate. There is a contest going on here between God and Satan, and Job seems somehow aware of it. Job didn't say that God sent the adversity. He simply admitted that adversity and opposition are inevitable.

How we deal with this inevitable adversity when it comes is the core of the Christian life. It is easy to serve God when things are going right. This was Satan's premise for his argument with God. He felt Job's prosperity was covering up a soul of impiety. He told God point-blank, "Take away Job's stuff and his health, and you'll see. He'll reject you outright if you cut him off. Make it more difficult to serve you, and he'll stop serving you." God knew his servant better than Satan did. He knew that when things got tough, Job would still hold on to the truth of God. That was why God bragged about Job. He knew the true character that lay under the surface of Job's piety and prosperity.

Adversity is as sure in this life as the devil from which it comes. The question is, how will we deal with adversity when it comes? Will we curse God and reject Him, or will we bless Him

and press through, looking for the good that will ultimately come
from the adversity?

As New Testament believers, we are instructed to do more
than simply endure adversity; we are instructed to rejoice in it.
Look what the Apostles say.

> *In this you greatly rejoice,* even though now for a
> little while, if necessary, you have been distressed
> by various trials, so that the proof of your faith,
> being more precious than gold which is perishable,
> even though tested by fire, may be found to result
> in praise and glory and honor at the revelation of
> Jesus Christ. (1 Pet. 1:6–7 my emphasis)

> And not only this, but *we also exult in our
> tribulations,* knowing that tribulation brings
> about perseverance; and perseverance, proven
> character; and proven character, hope; and hope
> does not disappoint, because the love of God has
> been poured out within our hearts through the
> Holy Spirit who was given to us.
> (Rom. 5:3–5 my emphasis)

> *Consider it all joy, my brethren,* when you encounter
> various trials, knowing that the testing of your
> faith produces endurance. And let endurance have
> its perfect result, so that you may be perfect and
> complete, lacking in nothing. (James 1:2–4 my
> emphasis)

These verses have always been troubling to me. I have difficulty finding joy in tribulation. I often would rather sit in my ash pit in self-pity or lash out at those around me, like Job's wife. This is, I suspect, the knee-jerk reaction of most believers. But this is not the calling of Jesus's followers. We are called to find joy in trials, to exult in our tribulations, and to rejoice in distress. This is not easy. Job didn't do it fully. Like most of the followers of God on the Old Testament side of the cross, he didn't grasp the fullness of the scriptural message. However, he grasped enough to realize that God would bring him through.

Job didn't exult in tribulation, but we are instructed to find joy in trials. How do we do this? The way we do this is to first look upon this as an ongoing process. The testing and trials produce perseverance and endurance. Perseverance produces character, which in turn leads to hope, making our faith complete.

Peter uses a metaphor of gold being purified in a crucible to describe this faith. It is only in the heat of a crucible that gold can be refined. It is only in the heat of adversity that our faith can be hardened to bring glory to the Name of Jesus. The Old Testament prophets were also fond of this metaphor of the Spirit of God as a refiner's fire.

> "And I will bring the third part through the fire,
> Refine them as silver is refined,
> And test them as gold is tested.
> They will call on My name,
> And I will answer them;
> I will say, 'They are My people,'

And they will say, 'The Lord is my God.'"
(Zech. 13:9)

God places the ore of our faith in the crucible of adversity and then turns up the heat. As the heat rises, we are transformed from the raw materials of basic faith in Jesus to something pure and holy that is worthy of our Lord. The adversity is different for each of us. God knows how much heat to apply to our hearts to bring about the transformation that He desires. Each person's adversity is unique.

As the heat in the crucible is turned up, the dross, or undesirable material, begins to float to the top so that it can be removed and the gold can be purified. For our souls, this process can be quite painful (it was for Job), and it can get ugly at times. We indulge in self- pity. We lash out at those nearest to us. We even rail at God. But through it all, God holds us in the palm of His hand. The refiner doesn't just throw the gold directly into the fire; this would ruin His work. Instead, He places it in the crucible to protect it from the full intensity of the fire. This, His love expressed through His hand, is His crucible. It protects us from the fullness of the fire, limiting its effects to just enough to produce the desired result.

> *Who will separate us from the love of Christ?* Will tribulation, or distress, or persecution, or famine, or nakedness, or peril, or sword? Just as it is written,

"FOR YOUR SAKE WE ARE BEING PUT TO DEATH
ALL DAY LONG; WE WERE CONSIDERED AS
SHEEP TO BE SLAUGHTERED"

But in all these things we overwhelmingly
conquer through Him who loved us. For *I am
convinced that neither death, nor life, nor angels,
nor principalities, nor things present, nor things to
come, nor powers, nor height, nor depth, nor any
other created thing, will be able to separate us from
the love of God, which is in Christ Jesus our Lord.*
(Rom. 8:35–39 my emphasis)

Nothing can separate us from God's love. Paul's list is
quite comprehensive. Nothing means *no* thing. God's love is
unconditional, irrevocable, and unconquerable. He loves us and
is creating in us something that He desires. His tender mercies
are new every morning, and His crucible is ongoing. Both express
His love for us. Nothing in this world can withdraw His love
from us, and nothing can remove us from His crucible until He
has prepared us, transformed us, and completed His work in us.

We may not like the crucible, but it is necessary. The pit and
the prison were not pleasant, but they were necessary to transform
Joseph from a prideful, spoiled brat into a leader who would rescue
his family. The rejection of his brothers and opposition of Saul
were necessary to forge David into a leader who could carve out
a kingdom that would endure for centuries. The hardships that
the apostles and the Church fathers endured for their faith were

the crucible that established a church which would endure and grow through the millennia.

> Therefore we do not lose heart, but though our outer man is decaying, yet our inner man is being renewed day by day. *For momentary, light affliction is producing for us an eternal weight of glory far beyond all comparison,* while we look not at the things which are seen, but at the things which are not seen; for the things which are seen are temporal, but the things which are not seen are eternal.
> (2 Cor. 4:16–18 my emphasis)

Paul referred to his hardships as "light and momentary afflictions," but we know from his other writings that they could not have been easy. Paul was able to endure and rejoice in them because he knew that something more valuable was being produced. What was this valuable thing that God's crucible was producing in Paul and in us?

When an earthly refiner sits before the fire with his crucible, he watches it closely, controlling the heat and removing the dross. He keeps his eye on the metal in the crucible, and finally when he sees his own reflection in the molten metal, he knows that the refining process is complete; he can pour the metal into its mold. God is the same way. When He places us in His crucible, He keeps His eye on us until He sees His glory reflected in us. This is what He is producing in us: a reflection of His glory, love, mercy, faithfulness, goodness, kindness, patience, peace, and humility. When He sees all these qualities reflected in us, then His work is nearly finished.

Beloved, do not be surprised at the fiery ordeal among you, which comes upon you for your testing, as though some strange thing were happening to you; but to the degree that you share the sufferings of Christ, keep on rejoicing, so that also at the revelation of His glory you may rejoice with exultation. If you are reviled for the name of Christ, you are blessed, because the Spirit of glory and of God rests on you. Make sure that none of you suffers as a murderer, or thief, or evildoer, or a troublesome meddler; but *if anyone suffers as a Christian, he is not to be ashamed, but is to glorify God in this name.* (1 Pet. 4:12–16 my emphasis)

Bear in mind, though, that this refining process in us is an ongoing process. It rarely is done in a single session. For most of us, it takes years and has ups and downs. It is somewhat like the process of tempering a sword in which the steel is repeatedly heated and cooled to harden it and make it strong. Don't become discouraged if this process takes time and requires endurance. It is making you into what your Lord and Savior wants you to be. His tests are all open book, and He is willing to let you keep doing retakes until you get it right. He formed the world in six days but He is willing to take a lifetime to conform you to his image.

> "But He knows the way I take;
> When He has tried me, I shall come forth as gold.
> (Job 23:10)

It took twenty-one chapters and a lot of false accusations from his friends for Job to come to this bit of revelation. But God's testimony about Job is still this: "In all this Job did not sin with his lips." (Job 2:10) Job did not attribute the evil to God, but he recognized that God allowed the evil to come upon him to test him and refine the gold of his character. We too can expect adversity in our lives, but we can allow a loving creator to use the destructive in our lives to produce something constructive. He uses Satan's attempts at destruction to allow His reflected image to shine forth through us.

He began this process in me years ago, and it is still ongoing. He first allowed Satan to take away the things that I valued the most so that I would be able to recognize the things that He values the most.

NUGGET #3

My Servant

"But it is still my consolation,
And I rejoice in unsparing pain,
That I have not denied the words of the Holy One."
(Job 6:10)

Job's biggest challenges were yet to come. The people closest to him were the ones who had the most effect on his life. His wife urged him to give up the fight, quit, lie down, and die. Then his friends showed up.

We first meet them at the end of chapter 2. They are apparently Job's best friends, and at this moment, they are his only friends. Everyone else has abandoned Job in his distress. We have seen this in our own lives. Human nature seems to be either to avoid someone in trouble, or worse, to kick him while he's down. At least Job's friends didn't abandon him.

They seem to be at a loss for words at first. I don't know anyone who could sit with someone in mourning for a week without saying a word. My nature is to try to say something, anything to fill the void and try to bring comfort. Maybe they were shocked at his appearance or appalled at the depths to which he had sunk. Maybe they feared that their own fate might someday be the same.

Like Job, these men were leaders in their community, respected and honored for their success and wisdom. But they were dumbfounded when they encountered their old friend. They didn't know what to say, and so they said nothing. I think we could learn from this. Sometimes we don't need to say anything; we simply need to let someone who is in trouble know that at least someone still cares. They mourned over him, they mourned for him, and they shared in his mourning, tearing their robes and throwing the ashes on their own heads. One can never say that these men didn't care. They cared to the point of stepping away from their comfortable lives to try to bring comfort to Job.

Then to their astonishment, their friend begins to speak. Like George Bailey in the classic Christmas movie *It's a Wonderful Life*, Job wishes that he had never been born. He reasons that all this trouble would have been avoided if he had been a stillborn child. Then he would have gone straight to a resting place where no trouble could befall him. (Job 3: 1-13)

> "There the wicked cease from raging,
> And there the weary are at rest.
> "The prisoners are at ease together;
> They do not hear the voice of the taskmaster.
> "The small and the great are there,
> And the slave is free from his master. (Job 3:17–19)

These words do not seem unfamiliar to the modern believer. Many of us have hoped for an escape from our troubles. We may even have silently asked God, "Why don't you just take me on home? Then my troubles will be over." We long for the sweet escape of the rapture and heaven, but we know that we cannot exit this world until God's timing and His purpose are fulfilled. Paul lived and wrote about this tearing of the soul.

> But I am hard-pressed from both directions, having the desire to depart and be with Christ, for that is very much better; yet to remain on in the flesh is more necessary for your sake. (Phil. 1:23–24)

Job is tired of the fight. We can all identify with this. He simply wants to be at peace. He wants the trouble to be over, but he knows that his life is not yet finished. Like Paul, he has more to accomplish.

His friends are shocked to hear this discouragement coming from Job, who has been one to strengthen and encourage others. Eliaphaz, the first to speak, tells him so.

> "Behold you have admonished many,
> And you have strengthened weak hands.
> "Your words have helped the tottering to stand,
> And you have strengthened feeble knees. (Job 4:3–4)
> He chides Job,

> "But now it has come to you, and you are impatient;

It touches you, and you are dismayed.
"Is not your fear of God your confidence,
And the integrity of your ways your hope? (Job
4:5–6)

Job's "comforters" have received a lot of criticism over the years, and most of it is warranted, but occasionally they do have a bit of wisdom. Here, Eliaphaz reminds Job of the position that he has held in the community: one of leadership and encouragement. Job has helped many people who have been in similar situations, in ash pits of their own. He has strengthened them, encouraged them, and helped them to stand on their own. Eliaphaz reminds Job of where he has been and chides him because Job thought that he was somehow immune to trouble. Then he reminds Job of the source of the help that Job has offered to the community. This source is in Job's integrity, fear of God, and the hope that filled his life. This is what had enabled Job to be a leader, an encourager, and a strengthener. Now, when the hope is dimmed by trouble, Job is giving up. He encourages Job to continue to hope. Eliaphaz has been gently chiding Job and encouraging him, but then he takes a hard left turn.

"Remember now, who ever perished being
innocent?
Or where were the upright destroyed?
"According to what I have seen, those who plow
iniquity
And those who sow trouble harvest it. (Job 4:7–8)

In one breath, he speaks of Job's integrity and fear of God. In the next, he says the calamity that has befallen Job is as a result of Job's sin. He even claims to have received this revelation in a dream.

> "Now a word was brought to me stealthily,
> And my ear received a whisper of it.
> "Amid disquieting thoughts from the visions of
> the night,
> When deep sleep falls on men. (Job 4:12–13)

Eliaphaz is telling Job that his trouble is of his own doing, and at the end of his speech, he tells Job that if he had been doing right, that if he had heeded God's warnings, then God would have protected him from this calamity.

> "Behold, how happy is the man whom God reproves,
> So do not despise the discipline of the Almighty.
> "For He inflicts pain, and gives relief;
> He wounds, and His hands also heal.
> "From six troubles He will deliver you,
> Even in seven evil will not touch you. (Job 5:17–19)

Yes, God punishes and will punish sin. It is intolerable to Him. But not every disaster is brought about by sin in the subject's life. Job is a prime example of this. It is very clear that the trouble was not brought about by sin on Job's part. Quite the contrary— this trouble was as a result of Job's integrity. We must be careful not to make snap assessments of situations in which we and others find ourselves. Truly, trouble can come to us as a result of sin, and it can come as a way of testing and proving us and our integrity.

However, Job is still deep in his sorrow. His wife has abandoned him, his fortunes have turned, his family is dead, and his only friends are accusing him of being to blame for all of it. It is almost too much to bear. He cries out,

> "Oh that my request might come to pass,
> And that God would grant my longing!
> "Would that God were willing to crush me,
> That He would loose His hand and cut me off!"
> (Job 6:8–9)

He wouldn't abandon his integrity to curse God and die, but it seems he is willing and somewhat eager to accept death if God would just do it Himself. This is echoed in Paul's sentiments.

> For indeed in this house we groan, longing to be clothed with our dwelling from heaven. (2 Cor. 5:2)

> But I am hard-pressed from both directions, having the desire to depart and be with Christ, for that is very much better; yet to remain on in the flesh is more necessary for your sake. (Phil. 1:23–24)

> For we are His workmanship, created in Christ Jesus for good works, which God prepared beforehand so that we would walk in them. (Eph. 2:10)

Both Job and Paul were willing to leave this decision in God's hands. Job would not curse God and die. Paul was willing to go on groaning in his earthly tent because he knew that there were works that were yet unfinished. Job also knew his work was not done.

> "But it is still my consolation,
> And I rejoice in unsparing pain,
> That I have not denied the words of the Holy One."
> (Job 6:10)

Job held tight to his integrity through his pain. He accepted that God was not yet finished with him and there was still much to accomplish. His family was gone, his wealth was gone, and his friends were kicking him while he was down. All he had was the words of God: "consider My servant, Job." He held on to his God and the truth of His word. Sometimes this is all we have left, but we must hold on to this. What is *this*, though? To what words of the holy one should I hold fast? To what words should you hold?

The only words Job had and needed were these: "consider My servant." The only thing Job needed was his identity in God and a knowledge of how his God regarded him. God spoke of Job as "My servant." This phrase has two parts: the noun, *servant*, and the possessive pronoun, *My*.

The noun *servant* means someone who is hired or bound to serve someone or something. The servant doesn't serve to please himself but to please the master. This was Job's identity: God's servant. He served God not just when things were going good, but all the time. He served God when he was prosperous, offering sacrifices in case one of his children had sinned. He served God when things weren't going well, when Satan was afflicting him with loss and sickness, saying,

> "Naked I came from my mother's womb,
> And naked I shall return there.
> The Lord gave and the Lord has taken away.
> Blessed be the name of the Lord." (Job 1:21)

Job recognized that he was the servant and God was the master. All that Job had came from God and through God's grace. But still, there is that other word: *My*. God identifies Job as a servant for sure, but He goes further than that. He says, "My servant, Job." Job belongs to God! This possessive pronoun is powerful in the hands of almighty God. It demonstrates the nature of their relationship. God is the possessor of heaven and earth, the creator of the entire universe, but His ownership of His people (including Job) is special. He identifies Job as someone special who belongs to God. Job belonged to God, and that is the source of the conflict between God and Satan here. Satan wanted what God had. From the beginning, this was the problem. Satan wanted the worship that was due God.

We too belong to God. Like Job, we have a special relationship with our owner and creator. If we stop to think about it, this relationship of belonging to Him is awe-inspiring. How is it that God owns us? What does it mean for us?

We belong to God because Jesus purchased our lives on the cross, redeeming us from a life of sin and shame, buying us back from the slavery of sin, and purchasing our souls with His precious blood.

For you have been bought with a price: therefore
glorify God in your body. (1 Cor. 6:20)

Knowing that you were not redeemed with
perishable things like silver or gold from your
futile way of life inherited from your forefathers,
but with precious blood, as of a lamb unblemished
and spotless, the blood of Christ. (1 Pet. 1:18–19)

"Worthy are You to take the book and to break its
seals; for You were slain, and purchased for God
with Your blood men from every tribe and tongue
and people and nation." (Rev. 5:9)

This servant/possessor relationship makes us unique in all of
creation. God gave up Himself in the person of Jesus, the Son, to
purchase us from the bondage of sin and death. In doing so, He
takes rule over us and also takes responsibility for our well-being.

Let's see if we can put this relationship into terms that will be
easier to grasp. At the time of this writing, I own a 1999 model
pickup truck. It is mine. I bought it with money that I earned, and
I have the right to say where it goes and who drives it. I can loan
it to a friend, but I am still responsible for any damage it might
cause if my friend wrecks it. I am responsible to pay the taxes and
license fees that are due each year on the truck. I am responsible to
maintain it. If I don't change the oil and check the pressure in the
tires, and it malfunctions, it is my responsibility to have it repaired.
Ownership of this vehicle is a privilege and a responsibility.

This example is but a dim reflection of God's ownership of

His people. We belong to Him. He has the right to say where we go and what we do. He paid the ultimate price for us: His own righteous blood. He also takes responsibility for our well-being. He has promised to provide for our needs from His riches. He takes responsibility to take us through the refiner's fire of life, and to see to our education and maturation as believers.

The analogy breaks down a little bit at this point, though. Although my truck is mostly in my control, it is still subject to circumstances and road conditions, other drivers' actions, and such. God allows us to have a free will as He works out His plans in our lives. He uses the circumstances in our lives and the actions of others to lead us in the direction He wants. My truck is an inanimate machine, whereas we Christians are individuals with souls and wills that God allows us to exercise, hopefully in concert with His plans to bring us to maturity and fruitfulness in His kingdom.

This relationship sets His people apart as something special in all of His creation. We are unique and distinct from the rest of His creation simply because He paid for us to redeem us from the penalty of sin with His own precious blood on the cross. Job was His servant and we too belong to Him. This is our identity in the new birth through belief and profession of faith in the work that Jesus did on the cross. We are his! We are to serve Him, and He takes responsibility for us.

NUGGET #4

Hope

"Though He slay me,
I will hope in Him. Nevertheless, I will argue
my ways before Him." (Job 13:15)

When things don't go as we wish, we often cry out to God as Job did. His grief was too much to bear alone. His friends accused him of falsehood and disobedience to God. His wife told him that he would be better off dead, and that his service to God was pointless. Job only had one place to turn: the Almighty. He would plead his case before the throne of God.

He placed his trust and hope in the eternal justness of God. He knew in his heart that God would uphold the cause of the righteous.

If you are pure and upright,
Surely now He would rouse Himself for you
And restore your righteous estate. (Job 8:6)

When Bildad spoke these words, he was mocking Job. He insisted that Job's troubles were all his of his own making and that God was punishing Job for his sins. In fairness to Bildad, he didn't see the battle going on in the heavenly realm, as we do. Thank God that, in hindsight, we do have the benefit of seeing more of the picture than the patriarchs saw. Even in his shortsighted position, Bildad could see some truth. The Righteous God is an upholder of righteous men.

> For the Lord is righteous, He loves righteousness;
> The upright will behold His face. (Ps. 11:7)
> The eyes of the Lord are toward the righteous
> And His ears are open to their cry. (Ps. 34:15)

Job took the one kernel of truth in Bildad's mocking and ran with it. He would put himself in the court of the Lord. He would plead his case before the only just and fair judge. He prepared his case and proclaimed his innocence. This was risky business. If he was found guilty, the penalty could be death. Job voices this possibility when he cries out, "Though he slay me," but completing his thought is, "yet will I hope in Him." This hope was not just some "pie in the sky" wishing. It was an abiding belief in the eternal, just nature of God. God is the God of hope.

> Now may the God of hope fill you with all joy and
> peace in believing, so that you will abound in hope
> by the power of the Holy Spirit. (Rom. 15:13)

What is hope? Job said, "I will hope in Him." Paul called the Lord "the God of hope." What is hope, and in whom or what should we place our hope?

Hope is defined in the dictionary as confident expectation or likelihood of success. Often we define it differently. Hope to most of us seems to be wishful thinking. We wish for good things with no real expectation of receiving them. We do not really see a difference between hoping and wishing. We say, "I hope it doesn't rain tomorrow," but we really have no expectation of our hope being fulfilled.

The biblical concept of hope is different from our wishful thinking. It is based in an abiding belief that God is good and is on our side, working things out for the ultimate good of His chosen people. Even when things seem to be going badly, we can have a hope in the goodness of God that He will cause things to work out for the best.

> And we know that God causes all things to work together for good to those who love God, to those who are called according to His purpose. (Rom. 8:28–29)

This is one of the most influential verses in my life. When things go wrong, I can always remember this verse. It says that all things work together for God's eternal purpose. Whether they seem to be good or bad, blessing or cursing, helping or harming, they still work together for the ultimate good of God's people who love Him. This verse is the greatest statement of the source of hope for Christians everywhere. In the hands of our mighty God, everything, whether intended for good or evil, is transformed into a force for our ultimate benefit. This is the source of our hope.

My mother has always been one of the most influential people in my life. This is no great revelation. It is the same case for most of us, but she is still a special source of hope in my life. She doesn't think she's nearly as brilliant as she actually is. Because she hasn't memorized entire books of the Bible, she downplays her own understanding of scripture, but she has done more than most to take the scriptures into her heart and make them a part of her.

When I was a teenager and things were not going my way, I would become frustrated and feel that things would never be right again. My mother would simply tell me, "It's all going to work out in the end." She didn't beat me over the head with the scriptures. She reassured me that everything would work out for the best. And it did! She has this verse down in her heart so deeply that she is sure things will work out for the best if we trust God and let Him work out His plan in our lives. When I read this verse, I hear her voice reassuring me that things will work out for the best.

This is how our hope in God should be. No matter what happens, whether we live or die, whether or not we succeed in this endeavor, we always have this hope from our God. All things (that's right: all means all—good things or bad) work together for good. If the Almighty strikes Job dead, or if He heals Job and restores his fortunes, it will all work out for the ultimate good.

Notice that I started that last paragraph with a disclaimer. Although the paragraph above represents the ideal of what my hope should be, my life often does not look like this at all. I question whether things will work out for the best. Oh, I know that everything will be all right in the "sweet by and by." I know that I will eventually get to heaven, and at Jesus's side, everything will be just peachy. But in the here and now, when things are not going my way, I can lose hope for anything good to come of my trouble. This is a very natural, human reaction to adverse circumstances. I react in this way less now than I did before, but that lack of hope is still there, crouching at the door and waiting to draw me in.

I wrote before about a softball injury which had left me unable to work even in the unlikely event that I would be able to find a job in the economic downturn of those days. I can look back now and see the hope that was there, but then I had little hope.

After this accident, I saw no light at the end of the tunnel. I was angry at people around me who had seemingly conspired against me to deny me opportunity. I was angry at God, who, though capable, seemed uncaring about my fate. I was disappointed, disillusioned, and desperate. I was ready to grasp at anything like a drowning man.

Then along came a fellow who promised to show me a way that I could become financially independent.

What he showed me was one of the many multilevel marketing programs that were very common in those days. He showed me how, if I got involved and began selling his products, and then I got other people involved underneath me, I could have the income and lifestyle that I always thought I should have. Their motto was, "See you on the beaches of the world." I did not think I was a very good salesman, but the initial investment was small, and I had little to lose, so I was in.

I feel the need to mention that I am telling this story for a purpose, which will become more apparent as I go on. I do not recommend this path to success. This is an example of how God has used the circumstances in my life, many of them of my own making, to accomplish His goal. Some people have become very successful in this type of business, but God had another plan for it in my life.

His plan was not to use this business model to prosper me, but to use the experience to mold me into someone that He would find more useful in His kingdom. This experience forced me to lay aside my introverted nature and get past my fear of public speaking, because I was expected to invite people to presentations in which the business model would be presented and they would be given an opportunity to participate. I was also expected to be able to present the business to others myself. Although my outward success at this was not wildly fruitful, the inward change that it wrought was substantial. I found that I was able to talk to people individually and in groups. I will never consider myself a great, dynamic orator, but I am capable of getting my ideas across to people in a clear and concise manner. This experience is not the only way that this developed in my life, but God used it mightily to bring about a change by forcing me out of my shell.

One way that God used this period of my life was through the other people who were involved in the same business with me. It was not a Christian business, per se, but many of the leaders in the organization were Christians and recommended that all their distributors be involved and active in their local churches. To be fair, this was probably because they viewed the churches as a fertile ground for recruitment, but at their urging, my wife and I became more active in our local church. We were never successful at recruiting there, but we did build relationships during that time that are still active and vital today. The people of that church embodied the notion of God using all things to work together for the ultimate good of His chosen people. Their positive outlook reflected the belief that we as Christians are "more than conquerors through Christ Jesus." We were hearing and receiving the word of God into our lives, and we established relationships with people who believed it and were doing their best to live the Christian life. This does not mean that they never had troubles. Instead, when they had troubles, they trusted God to bring them through. It was the combination of these things that began the process of developing the bitter, frustrated introvert into who I am today.

The other way that He used this time was through books. The leaders of our organization recommended that we read inspirational and motivational books. I had no problem with this. I am a reader and come from a family of readers. If I could become rich by reading books, I was in, and so I dug into the reading list.

At the head of this reading list was the Bible, but it also included positive thinking type books by authors like Zig Ziglar and Dale Carnegie. Many of the books were by Christian authors like Tim Le Haye and James Dobson. As I read these books, especially the Bible, my thinking started to change. I developed something that had been hiding down deep in my life: a little thing called hope. I began to believe that God was actively at work in my life and that He had some sort of a plan for me.

The Lord used this time and the tool of that business to start a process that is still ongoing today. He planted the seeds of hope and faith in my life. They were small at first, like seeds tend to be, and the seedlings were spindly and weak, but they were there, and He was going to see that they grew. His intention was not for me to be a financial success in that business, but for that business to be successful in me. As I said before, I do not recommend this path to success for everyone. Some people have been very successful in this type of business, earning substantial incomes and living their dream on the beaches of the world. In my own life, God used this time and this tool to bring about a change to a positive frame of mind, especially where He is concerned. I have no doubt that everything will work out to produce His best in His people. This is the hope that we all have and can hold tightly. He takes all the circumstances of our lives—the good, the bad, and the things that are neither good nor bad but are simply something that He can use to accomplish His purpose in us—and He causes them all to work together for the common good of His called, chosen people, both collectively and individually. This is what the apostle is telling us in Romans 8:28. All these things can be used by God to work together for the greater good.

Thanks, Mom. You have no idea how I have held on to this teaching throughout my life. Thanks to the many positive and encouraging people who have met with me on the way. Most of you do not even know the great good you have accomplished, but I do. And thank you, God, for placing this hope in all Your people and allowing it to express Your nature as the God of hope. It really will all work out in the end.

NUGGET #5

Our Advocate

"Even now, behold, my witness is in heaven,
And my advocate is on high. (Job 16:19)

Job spends most of his time complaining about his troubles, and justifiably so, but occasionally he hits on one of these prophetic gems that make his trip to the ash pit worthwhile. Job's words take us into the heavenly realms and give us a glimpse of what is really going on there.

Job had longed for someone to be his advocate before God and judge him righteous. He was looking for someone who could represent him but no one was worthy of that honor.

> "For He is not a man as I am that I may answer Him,
> That we may go to court together.
> "There is no umpire between us,
> Who may lay his hand upon us both." (Job 9:32–33)

Here, Job speaks from the depths of his pain, saying, "I need an advocate, someone to intercede with God on my behalf." Job is crying out prophetically for someone to set him free from sin and death, from sickness and suffering, from accusation and guilt. He is looking for a deliverer.

Job knew that he was unworthy to enter into the holy presence of God to plead his case. He longed to do this and proclaim his innocence, but he knew that he needed an advocate to go before God for him. He needed someone to represent him and speak on his behalf. He needed the Messiah, a deliverer, an advocate, an umpire to speak up and tell God that he was being treated unfairly and did not deserve the suffering that he was experiencing. But he instinctively knew that there was no one, not even Job himself, who was worthy to speak his case before God. He had to look further than his own existence. Job looked ahead and into the heavenlies, and he saw Jesus interceding with the Father for him and for us.

The idea of a personal deliverer was not as concrete in Job's patriarchal period as it became later. The earliest reference to a deliverer in the Old Testament is the Genesis 3 reference to the "seed of woman" who would crush the head of the serpent, Satan. By the time of the Exodus, the idea of a personal deliverer was cemented in Israelite thinking. They were ready to accept Moses as their deliverer from Pharaoh's bondage. Later Jewish readers would see this prophetic reference by Job as indicating the expected Messiah or Anointed One. It is clear from later writings that the Israelites were expecting a savior to arise and intercede for them with their God.

Yet He Himself bore the sin of many,

And interceded for the transgressors. (Isa. 53:12b)

The Jews of the Babylonian exile expected to be delivered from their captivity and returned to their land. The Roman-occupied Jews expected a Messiah to arise and throw off the bondage of Rome. Even today, Jews look to a future Messiah to deliver them from their troubles.

The word *Messiah* translates into Greek as Christ. It is clear to Christians in hindsight that Job's words are one of the earliest references to our savior, Jesus, and His role as our advocate on high.

> My little children, I am writing these things to you so that you may not sin. And if anyone sins, we have an Advocate with the Father, Jesus Christ the righteous. (1 John 2:1)

> Christ Jesus is He who died, yes, rather who was raised, who is at the right hand of God, who also intercedes for us. (Rom 8:34b)

> For Christ did not enter a holy place made with hands, a mere copy of the true one, but into heaven itself, now to appear in the presence of God for us. (Heb. 9:24)

Although Job had no worthy advocate in his present to plead his case because Jesus had yet to sacrifice Himself and rise from the dead, he could look prophetically into the heavenlies and see his advocate, the preexistent and future Messiah, Jesus. No one is more worthy than Jesus, the sinless Lamb of God. When Satan, the false accuser, spoke his condemning lies, Jesus was there before the throne as Job's advocate, speaking on Job's behalf. When that same liar accuses us, the same Jesus is there, reminding the Father and the liar that his blood has bought us and made us clean.

Jesus is our advocate at the Father's side and much more. Job sought an advocate to present his innocence before the Almighty. We have an advocate who does much more than that. Jesus doesn't just plead the case for our innocence. He took our sin upon Himself and took it to the cross, receiving our punishment in His own body. Then day by day, He takes his own sinless holiness and dresses us in it, presenting us before the Father, holy and righteous, justified and acquitted of all charges. This is the essence of Christianity.

> He made Him who knew no sin to be sin on our
> behalf, so that we might become the righteousness
> of God in Him.
> (2 Cor. 5:21)

This is what sets Christianity apart from any other religion or belief system. Religions like paganism and shamanism use ritual and sacrifice to appease the "gods" and avoid their wrath. These belief systems are based on man reaching up to the "gods" and trying to satisfy them. Islam is based on men reaching up to Allah and attempting to please him. Judaism was originally based on the covenant relationship between the tribe of Israel and God and cemented by the animal sacrifice and obedience to Torah. While it is rooted in the covenant it is often more about ethnicity and moral philosophy and is still dependent on man's observance of God's laws. While Judaism and the covenant relationship between God and Israel are the foundation of Christianity, it is still only a shadow of what was to come.[3] Philosophies like Buddhism and humanism expect men to improve themselves and are largely disappointing because we are unable to improve ourselves on a consistent basis. Christianity turns all this around. God sacrificed Himself, in the person of Jesus, to pay our sin debt and redeem us from the curse of sin and death. God Himself has become our advocate before His own throne of righteous judgment on our behalf. Then, God Himself takes on the job of molding us and improving us into what He sees as our best destiny. This a total reversal of the usual religious or philosophical paradigm.

Job looked up into the heavenlies and saw Jesus, our advocate and his, and he rejoiced. We have an advocate to speak for us and plead our case, to live as one of us and die for us, to redeem us from the depth of sin and make us righteous and acceptable to God. This is our savior, our advocate, our Lord, Jesus.

Like Job, I was looking for someone to plead my case. I wanted someone to blame for my troubles. It was easy to blame people around me for my problems because they were right there, and I could see them. Like Job, I lashed out at others and accused them of being useless and false, and even conspiring to hold me back. I needed an advocate to plead my case, but I also needed a change of heart and perspective.

In my gloom and despondency, I know that I actually wished these people removed from their positions of power so they could no longer oppose me. I don't recall actually praying for this, but in my heart, I know this is what I wanted. When I later learned that one of the people whom I believed was opposing me had died, my initial reaction was one of relief that now maybe I wouldn't be held down anymore. I know this is not a very Christian attitude, but let's face it: I wasn't a very good Christian at the time. I did feel sorrow for his family and hope that he did not wind up in hell's fires. Even at my lowest, I would not have wished that on anyone.

Did my wishes (for truly even my prayers were little more than wishes at that time) cause this man's death? I don't think so. I believe even if I had prayed that way, God, in His mercy, would have answered that prayer with a resounding no. But He did use this as a way to show me the evil that was lurking at the door to my own heart, waiting to drag me into its trap of bitterness and hate. When I recognized this attitude in myself, I found myself repenting of my hate and anger toward this man and all the others whom I had seen as treating me badly. This was only the first step in a long journey of learning to desire peace and reconciliation, mercy and forgiveness, truth and light. Through this journey, I have been learning that the true battle is "against evil rulers and authorities of the unseen world, against mighty powers in this dark world, and against evil spirits in the heavenly places."[4]

My battle was not with the people around me, but with the sinful nature and the evil thoughts that I chose to entertain. On the other side of this battle are the promises of God and His mercy and grace.

At the time, I couldn't see was what was going on in the heavenly realm, and how it could have implications in the earthly life. I originally only saw my battle as one on this earth with human individuals and human institutions. In heaven's courts, the battle was going on between my advocate, Jesus, and my accuser, Satan. In the spiritual realm, the battle was going on between me and the powers of darkness.

Jesus was interceding for me even when I didn't know it. He was pleading my case before the throne of God and asking that I be strengthened so that I could resist temptation and learn to forgive and be reconciled to those who might do me wrong. At the same time, the accuser was spouting his lies and sending his minions to harass and harry me with whatever they could find at hand.

I battle on, and dear reader, so will you. I have not arrived at the pinnacle of perfection in this yet, and likely I will not until Jesus takes me home, but I know that Jesus is faithful and true, and He will continue to be my advocate before the throne. He will continue to pray that the Holy Spirit will strengthen and embolden me to continue to resist the devil and his schemes and attacks. My prayer, and more important, Jesus's prayer, is that you too will be strengthened and empowered to resist the devil and his schemes and emerge victorious.

NUGGET #6

Our Redeemer

"As for me, I know that my Redeemer lives,
And at the last He will take His stand on the earth."
(Job 19:25)

We return now to our original pattern. Job's friends accuse him of wrongdoing. Job proclaims his innocence and states that he has been treated unfairly. He laments his circumstance and says that it seems that God no longer cares for him.

> "He breaks me down on every side, and I am gone;
> And He has uprooted my hope like a tree." (Job
> 19:10)

Job cried out that he has nothing left—no family, no fortune, and especially no hope. His fortunes were gone. His position in the community was lost. His friends loathed him. Even his wife couldn't stand him. When his family was destroyed, he lost the hope of immortality through his

progeny. Job felt that he had nothing left of expectation except
the grave.

> "All my associates abhor me,
> And those I love have turned against me." (Job 19:19)

At first, he lashed out at his friends who had been treating him
unfairly, accusing him of sins he had not committed.

> "How long will you torment me and crush me
> with words?" (Job 19:2)

Then he told them it was not any of their business. If Job had
sinned, it was between himself and God.

> "Even if I have truly erred, my error lodges with me."
> (Job 19:4)

Next, he blamed God for his misfortune. He launched into a
lament of several verses that complain God had turned against Job
and destroyed everything in his life, turning his friends against
him, causing his servants to ignore him, and even causing his
family members who were left to turn on him.

> Know then that God has wronged me
> And has closed His net around me. (Job 19:6)

> "He has removed my brothers far from me, and my
> acquaintances are completely estranged from me."
> (Job 19:13)

"I call to my servant, but he does not answer. I
have to implore him with my mouth. My breath
is offensive to my wife, and I am loathsome to my
own brothers."
(Job 19:16–17)

"Pity me, pity me, O you my friends, for the hand
of God has struck me." (Job 19:21)

In the middle of this pity party, Job experienced revelation
again. While he was lamenting all that he had lost, from
somewhere deep in Job's knowledge of God, he received a vision
of things to come.

"As for me, I know that my Redeemer lives, and
at the last He will take His stand on the earth.
Even after my skin is destroyed, yet from my flesh
I shall see God; Whom I myself shall behold and
whom my eyes will see and not another. My heart
faints within me!" (Job 19:25–27)

Job identifies his God as a redeemer, one who buys something
back that has been lost or stolen, one who avenges a wrong, and
one who makes something acceptable or restores one's reputation.
Job is expecting God to do all these things for him. He believes
that God will restore his fortunes and bring him out of his
predicament, restoring the reputation that had been lost, making
him acceptable to God, who had somehow turned against him.

Job and the other Old Testament faithful only saw this in shadow as they waited to experience it for themselves. However, we are experiencing the redemption of our souls and will, along with Job, witness God in resurrected bodies.

> All these died in faith, without receiving the promises, but having seen them and having welcomed them from a distance, and having confessed that they were strangers and exiles on the earth. (Heb. 11:13)

> In Him we have redemption through His blood, the forgiveness of our trespasses, according to the riches of His grace which He lavished on us. (Eph. 1:7–8)

We understand this redemption of God much more clearly from our side of the cross. We have been redeemed from the bondage of sin and shame, from the curse of death and destruction by Jesus's sacrifice on the cross. We are made acceptable to God by the atoning blood of Jesus and its cleansing power. We have been set free by our redeemer who lives. Job and Abraham could only see this from a distance and rejoice (John 8:56). We live it every day of our lives.

Job's vision extended far beyond the cross, though.

> And at the last He will take His stand on the earth. (Job 19:25b)

By faith, Job knew that his redeeming God would still be

standing when the end came. He looked beyond the troubles of this life and saw a triumphant and victorious Jesus standing at the end of the age. When the troubles had passed and the devil was vanquished, the redeemer would still be standing. This was Job's hope and ours too. One of the attributes of an Old Testament redeemer was that of an avenger.[5] This is the picture of Jesus standing at the end of the age which Job saw. Job saw the Jesus of Revelation triumphing over the beast, the false prophet, Satan, and his fallen angels, casting them in the lake of fire. But he saw even more.

> Even after my skin is destroyed, yet from my flesh
> I shall see God; Whom I myself shall behold and
> whom my eyes will see and not another. (Job
> 19:26–27a)

Job also expected a bodily resurrection in which he would see God with physical eyes. Job saw this from the patriarchal, time but in Jesus's day there were many, especially in the Sadducee party, who denied that there would be a resurrection. When God brought Jesus back from the dead, he showed definitively that there is a resurrection. We will see God with resurrected eyes. We can also expect a bodily resurrection.

> Behold, I tell you a mystery; we will not all sleep,
> but we will all be changed, in a moment, in the
> twinkling of an eye, at the last trumpet; for the
> trumpet will sound, and the dead will be raised
> imperishable, and we will be changed. (1 Cor.
> 15:51–53)

> But our citizenship is in heaven. And we eagerly
> await a Savior from there, the Lord Jesus Christ,
> who, by the power that enables him to bring
> everything under his control, will transform our
> lowly bodies so that they will be like his glorious
> body. (Phil. 3:20–21 NIV)

This hope of a resurrection is what drives us forward. We know that at some time the trouble of this life will come to an end, and we will finally be transformed into the fullness of the new creation that was begun in us at the new birth. Our greatest hope is that this world and all its trouble are only a temporary situation. They will someday come to an end for each of us, and we will step into the light of God's eternity.

Until then, though, we are still here in this world of trouble. How does this hope of a resurrection someday give us hope and empower us to live today? I knew that someday, I would go to live in heaven forever. But that still did not make the trouble that I was experiencing any less miserable.

This seems a little futile. Is the only hope that the resurrection gives us for the next life, and the best we can hope for is to someday make our escape from this life? If that is the case, then should we not simply hope to die the minute that Jesus saves us? I cannot count the times that I have prayed, "Lord, why don't you just take me home now and save both of us a lot of trouble?" This would be the easier path sometimes, but it is not the path He has chosen for His people. Paul wrote about this in his letter to the Philippians.

But I am hard-pressed from both directions, having
the desire to depart and be with Christ, for that is
very much better; yet to remain on in the flesh is
more necessary for your sake. (Phil. 1:23–25)

He considered going away to spend eternity with Jesus to be
the better outcome, but for the sake of the churches under his
care, he was willing to endure the hardships of this life. Paul's
goal was his eventual home with his Lord, but his mission was
to bring others into the knowledge of Jesus Christ so that they
too would be in that eventual home, and that they would in turn
bring others into that saving knowledge of Christ. This is how
we find the power and ability to endure the times of trouble. We
take our eyes off ourselves and look around us at a world that
desperately needs the same hope of resurrection and new life He
has given us. This inspired Paul to keep on, and it inspires us to
not give up the fight or give in to temptation. Paul wrote about
this in slightly different words.

It stands to reason, doesn't it, that if the alive-
and-present God who raised Jesus from the dead
moves into your life, he'll do the same thing in
you that he did in Jesus, bringing you alive to
himself? When God lives and breathes in you
(and he does, as surely as he did in Jesus), you
are delivered from that dead life. With his Spirit
living in you, your body will be as alive as Christ's!
(Rom. 8:11 MSG)

Look at that last line again. It reads, "Your body will be as alive as Christ's!" This is the great hope that the resurrection brings to us: besides an eternal life in heaven, we have been given a whole new life here in this world. That life is filled with opportunities and challenges, troubles and victories, blessings to be experienced and troubles to overcome. This is the nature of the new life that we experience in this world. He gives us this dual citizenship life that we live, knowing that our eventual home is not this world of trouble but a better, greater future life. At the same time, we're breathing new vitality, power, and meaning into the present life that we experience. This new life enables us to overcome the troubles that the devil throws our way by enabling us to take our focus off our own troubles and to focus (like Paul) on the needs of the hurting desperate people around us.

At this point in my story, I was not quite all the way to this great realization. I was still in the "Lord, take me home now" stage. It took years for this change of thinking to take root and bear the fruit of peace and encouragement to others that we see exemplified in Paul's life. To be fair, it took years for Paul to acquire these insights, but I am very glad he did. His journey through trouble and turmoil gives hope to me that I too can persevere and press on through the power of the resurrection in my life. If it works like this in Paul's life and mine, it can work in the life of others. Those who receive this new life in the Spirit will begin to be changed from within and will begin to change the world around them. This is the hope that the resurrection brings to us in this world.

NUGGET #7

The Living Word

"But He knows the way I take;
When He has tried me, I shall come forth as gold.
"My foot has held fast to His path;
I have kept His way and not turned aside.
"I have not departed from the command of His lips;
I have treasured the words of His mouth more than my
necessary food." (Job 23:10–12)

In chapter 22 Job's friends continue their accusations. They say that God has brought on calamity because of Job's sins. They even detail them, presumably so Job can repent. They accuse him of terrible things. They say that he is greedy, proud, and self-righteous; demands exorbitant interest of his kinsmen; takes food out of the mouths of widows and orphans; and takes the clothing off the backs of the needy. They say he is so proud that he believes even God cannot touch him, adding that he is unfaithful to God by failing to fulfill his vows. They assert that if Job will simply repent of his sin and turn back to God, then God will remove the punishment from him.

> "Can a vigorous man be of use to God,
> Or a wise man be useful to himself?
> "Is there any pleasure to the Almighty if you are righteous,
> Or profit if you make your ways perfect?
> "Is it because of your reverence that He reproves you,
> That He enters into judgment against you?" (Job 22:2–4)

> "Is not your wickedness great,
> And your iniquities without end?
> "For you have taken pledges of your brothers without cause,
> And stripped men naked.
> "To the weary you have given no water to drink,
> And from the hungry you have withheld bread."
> (Job 22:5–7)

> "You have sent widows away empty,
> And the strength of the orphans has been crushed.
> (Job 22:9)

Job doesn't respond to their accusations yet. His appeal is to the omniscient God. He says, "God himself knows the way I live my life. He alone can judge me. And, when He is finished I will come out of this refiner's furnace." He insists that he has not turned from God's path, and he has been faithful to God and generous and kind to his fellow men. He clings to his integrity and the word of God. These are all that he has left.

> "But He knows the way I take;
> When He has tried me, I shall come forth as gold.
> "My foot has held fast to His path;
> I have kept His way and not turned aside.
> "I have not departed from the command of His lips;
> I have treasured the words of His mouth more
> than my necessary food. (Job 23:10–12)

Then, he proclaims God's faithfulness.

> "But He is unique and who can turn Him?
> And what His soul desires, that He does.
> "For He performs what is appointed for me,
> And many such decrees are with Him." (Job 23:13–14)

Despite all that has happened, Job still has faith that God will do what is right and best for Job. This is faith.

It is easy to have faith when things are going well. It is another thing entirely to have faith when nothing seems to be right. This was the basis of Satan's challenge to God in the first place. He believed that Job's faith was only based in God's abundant blessing on Job's life. He said that Job would lose his faith when God withdrew His hand of protection. God knew better than that. God knew that Job would remain faithful, and He was willing to let Job go through the furnace to prove it.

This is the core of our faith also. When things are not going as we would wish, can we say, "For He performs what is appointed for me"? Can we say, "Blessed be the name of the Lord" when trouble with a capital T shows up? Can we truly say, "Though He slay me, I will hope in Him"? Jesus asked this same question in different words to Peter.

> As a result of this many of His disciples withdrew and were not walking with Him anymore. So Jesus said to the twelve, "You do not want to go away also, do you?" Simon Peter answered Him, "Lord, to whom shall we go? You have words of eternal life. "We have believed and have come to know that You are the Holy One of God." (John 6:66–69)

Peter's answer was the same as Job's. He had nowhere else to go. "To whom shall we go?" he asked. No one else could fill his need. The scribes and Pharisees were empty tombs; their hypocritical keeping of the letter of the law was a whitewash over their hardness of heart and uncaring attitude. The chief priests were political pawns of the Romans, going through the motions of ritual. Success in business was hollow and unsatisfying. Peter had tasted the words of eternal life, he had come to believe in Jesus, and nothing else could satisfy his desire. This is what Job said too.

"I have not departed from the command of His
lips; I have treasured the words of His mouth
more than my necessary food." (Job 23:12)

Once we have tasted of God's word and experienced the
gift of God's salvation through Jesus, there is no going back.
Nothing else in this world will satisfy our hunger for Him and
His word. This sustains us in the hard times, when we have
nothing else on which we can trust. We can lean on Jesus and
His words of eternal life. We can continue to follow Him even
when others might turn back. We realize that as bad as things
may become in this world, it is still only our temporary home.
Our eternal home is with Jesus, and nothing in this world can
compare to it. Nothing that Satan can throw at us can take
it away from us, because it is already bought and paid for by
the blood of Jesus. This is our safe harbor in life's storms, our
fortress against the enemy's attacks. The words of eternal life in
Jesus are what keep us from turning back and giving up.

This is how we as Christians respond to trouble, but we have
the written word of God, the Bible, to guide us. How was Job able
to say, "I have treasured the words of His mouth," when the Bible
as we know it was hundreds of years from being written down?
What are the words of His mouth to which Job refers? Job cannot
be referring to the five books of Moses when they had not been
written down yet. He could not possibly have been referring to the
New Testament word of God or the books of the prophets. These
did not exist in Job's patriarchal time period. Then how did Job
experience the words of God? Job professes faith in and a strong

desire for something that does not yet exist. This is a paradox. I know that I am asking a lot of questions, but it boils down to this.

What was the nature of Job's relationship with God? What did he have upon which he could believe?

> Because that which is known about God is evident within them; for God made it evident to them. For since the creation of the world His invisible attributes, His eternal power and divine nature, have been clearly seen, being understood through what has been made, so that they are without excuse. (Rom. 1:19)

That which is known about God is evident within them. Let that verse sink in a bit. Paul is writing here about people who have not yet come to a saving faith in Jesus. He says that even when they have not yet heard the gospel or been taught the Scriptures, there is a part of them that recognizes God's handiwork in the intricacy of nature's appearance. Additionally, they also understand that they have been created with a need to have an intimate relationship with their creator. They may not understand this need as such because the "god of this world" has blinded them, but they still need to fill this void somehow, and they will fill it with whatever is most available: drugs, promiscuity, money, or some vain philosophy. When we can look around us and see God's wonderful creation, or when we find the things of this world leave us feeling empty and unfulfilled, we recognize the hand of God and our need for His word in our lives. This is what Job was talking about. All of God's creation was spoken into being by His word, and this creation itself—from the largest galaxies to the intimate needs of His people—were created and spoken into being by His word.

> By faith we understand that the worlds were prepared by the word of God, so that what is seen was not made out of things which are visible. (Heb. 11:3)

The Greek word rendered in this verse as *the word* here is *rhema*. It means a word "that is spoken clearly and vividly, in unmistakable terms and in undeniable language. In the New Testament, *rhema* carries the idea of a *quickened word*."[6] This is the word of God come alive and active. He spoke, and the world came into existence. He breathed, and Adam became a living soul. This is the word that Job treasured in his heart, the living word of God becoming active and bringing life to Job's spirit. The living word of God was more valuable to Job than his daily bread.

Jesus knew this too. When he was in the wilderness, Satan tempted him with food, prosperity, and acclaim. Jesus countered the tempter with a word from God each time. This was a *rhema* word spoken in its proper time to produce the needed result. He was always ready to speak a well-timed word, and he valued this greatly. After He spoke to the Samaritan woman at the well, He told His disciples that He had tasted "food you know not of." The *rhema* word speaks life and power into the situations that arise. This is the word we should treasure too. It should always be ready on our lips in good times and bad.

Preach the word; be ready in season and out of season; reprove, rebuke, exhort, with great patience and instruction. (2 Tim. 4:2)

Stand therefore, having girded your waist with truth, having put on the breastplate of righteousness, and having shod your feet with the preparation of the gospel of peace; above all, taking the shield of faith with which you will be able to quench all the fiery darts of the wicked one. And take the helmet of salvation, and the sword of the Spirit, which is the *word of God*. (Eph. 6:14–18 NKJV my emphasis)

What is this word that Paul told Timothy to preach and that we are told is our sword to use to defeat the enemy? Is it this *rhema* word that we have been talking about? Is it the written word of God, the Bible? The short answer is it is both the written word of God and the word of God brought to life in us by the revelation of God. Let me explain how this works.

I grew up in a church that valued biblical teaching and understanding above all else. This seed was planted very early. Even though, like the prodigal son of Luke 15, I strayed from the way in my teenage and young adult years, when I returned from the far country as a young adult, I had a strong desire to live my life by the Bible, as I had been taught. When our pastor encouraged us to undertake a program in which, with a regular schedule of readings, we would read the entire Bible through in a year, the twin desires of Bible believer and lifelong reader latched on to the idea.[7]

As I was doing my reading, I had an ulterior, misguided, rather selfish motive. I was looking for some verse that I could use as a weapon to banish all the trouble from my life. "After all," I reasoned, "if the word of God is a sword, why shouldn't I use it to get rid of all the adverse circumstances that were active in my life and the lives of other believers?" I was looking for a silver bullet that I could use to overcome the enemy. But I continued reading, searching, and seeking. I knew it had to be in there somewhere. So read I did. Then, I read it through the next year too.

As I continued reading, I saw a pattern emerge. The word of God is not a tool to be used to get my way in life, but a way to find comfort and encouragement when things are not going the way that I want. It is a scalpel to remove pride and a hypodermic to inject faith into my life. Sometimes it is a weapon that I can wield to help me overcome the enemy of my soul and put temptation in its place, which is under the feet of Jesus. The written word of God is priceless, irreplaceable, and powerful. It is the blueprint for our existence and the owner's manual for the life He has given us.

Usually when I have read a book, I do not see a need to read it again. I know the story now. I have followed the twists and turns of the plot, got to know the characters, and know how the story ends. The Bible is not a book like that. Sure, it has great stories with memorable characters, and yes, I know how this story ends too, but it is much more than just another book to read. Every time I reread it, there is something new that I did not see before. Sometimes it is something in a verse that I have read many times, but I did not notice it before. Other times, a familiar verse comes to life in a new and different way to bring new insight. This is what that *rhema* word means.

It is alive. Its wisdom gets down deep inside and changes one from the inside out. It changed me, it is still changing me, and it will keep changing me until the day I step into eternity. I believe that even then, it will still keep changing me from glory to glory, because the Word of God is eternal and active.

> For the word of God is living and active and sharper than any two-edged sword, and piercing as far as the division of soul and spirit, of both joints and marrow, and able to judge the thoughts and intentions of the heart. (Heb. 4:12)

NUGGET #8

The Breath of God

"As God lives, who has taken away my right,
And the Almighty, who has embittered my soul,
For as long as life is in me,
And the breath of God is in my nostrils,
My lips certainly will not speak unjustly,
Nor will my tongue mutter deceit.
"Far be it from me that I should declare you right;
Till I die I will not put away my integrity from me.
"I hold fast my righteousness and will not let it go.
My heart does not reproach any of my days." (Job 27:2–6)

Job is once again responding to the accusations of his friends. At the end of chapter 25, Bildad has gone so far as to compare himself and Job to maggots and worms.

How much less man, that maggot,
And the son of man, that worm!" (Job 25:6)
Job's response is filled with sarcasm.

Then Job responded,
"What a help you are to the weak!
How you have saved the arm without strength!
"What counsel you have given to one without
wisdom!
What helpful insight you have abundantly
provided!
"To whom have you uttered words?
And whose spirit was expressed through you?"
(Job 26:1–4)

Job mocks Bildad as useless, without wisdom, and lacking insight. He even suggests that the source of Bildad's word was suspect, possibly even from Satan himself. He doesn't immediately refute Bildad's comparison, though. Job spends the rest of chapter 26 expounding on the greatness of God and his creative might.

"He stretches out the north over empty space
And hangs the earth on nothing." (Job 26:7)

"He has inscribed a circle on the surface of the waters
At the boundary of light and darkness." (Job 26:10)

Most modern scientists believe that before the enlightenment of the Renaissance and the brilliance of Galileo and Copernicus, everyone believed that the earth was flat and was held up by some giant. This is not what the Bible teaches. It is very clear that the ancients knew that the earth was a round sphere, and that it was held up in an apparent nothingness. This was written before the scientific and mathematical greats of Archimedes, Aristotle, Pythagoras, and Euclid. It took nearly two thousand years for Galileo and Copernicus to develop their models of the solar system, but Job's description of the round Earth hanging in space is a thousand years before the Greek fathers of science. If someone was teaching a flat earth model of the universe, he was not in agreement with the Bible.

> "The pillars of heaven tremble
> And are amazed at His rebuke.
> "He quieted the sea with His power,
> And by His understanding He shattered Rahab.
> "By His breath the heavens are cleared;
> His hand has pierced the fleeing serpent. (Job 26:11–13)

Job continues to proclaim God's greatness. He speaks of the power that God exerts over the heavens and the earth and all that is in them. Then he says this is just a tiny piece of how powerful and great God is.

> "Behold, these are the fringes of His ways;
> And how faint a word we hear of Him!
> But His mighty thunder, who can understand?"
> (Job 26:14)

It is possible that one might see in this proclamation of God's greatness the ability to see oneself and one's companions as comparable to worms when placed next to God, but Job has another idea entirely. He proclaims his steadfastness and refutes Bildad's argument at the same time.

> "As God lives, who has taken away my right,
> And the Almighty, who has embittered my soul,
> For as long as life is in me,
> And the breath of God is in my nostrils,
> My lips certainly will not speak unjustly,
> Nor will my tongue mutter deceit.
> "Far be it from me that I should declare you right;
> Till I die I will not put away my integrity from me.
> "I hold fast my righteousness and will not let it go.
> My heart does not reproach any of my days." (Job 27:2–6)

Job vows to hold to his integrity as long as "the breath of God is in [his] nostrils." With one breath, he says that God has allowed his life to become bitter, and that he has been denied justice by the Almighty. In the next breath, he acknowledges that his very breath came from that same God. Subtly, he is refuting Bildad's assertion that Job is a worm by pointing out that though God created both Adam and the worm, only Adam received the breath of God into his lungs. Adam was created to rule over the earth, not crawl around under it. It is this breath of God that sets Adam and his descendants apart from the maggots and worms. The spirit of God breathed life into Adam, and he became the pinnacle of God's creation.

As Christians, we carry that breath in our bodies. It sets us apart from the world. We were made a new creation in Christ, given a purpose, and empowered by the breath of the Almighty to do the works for which He has appointed us.

The Darwinists have tried in vain to drag the sons of Adam down to the level of the animals. They show us as descended from the worms that Bildad mentioned. They place those worms on the trunk of our family tree, but it is a tree that is rooted in unproven conjecture that sprang forth from a seed of nothingness. They place us on their tree of life, high in its branches as a pinnacle of their evolutionary process, but still a work in progress.

This last part is the half-truth that makes this philosophy palatable to some, even in Christian circles. Yes, we are works in progress. We are still growing, learning, maturing and becoming what we are. You could say that we are evolving, however that process of evolution in Christian believers is not the blind action of a philosophy of survival of the fittest, but the loving direction of a God who wants us to reach our true potential in Him. He guides us and prods us, and yes, sometimes He allows us to experience adversity and trouble to strengthen and refine us in their fires.

This process of the Christian life is somewhat like walking up the down escalator. We must keep on moving ahead, or else we naturally begin to fall behind. Job said, "I hold fast my righteousness and I will not let it go." This is a twofold process. First, we must hold on to our righteousness. We need to make an active effort to grasp onto the righteousness which is available to us. This is available to "whosoever will" (Rom. 10:13). We must recognize our need, repent of our sin, and then call out to Him asking him to save us. As we do this we are grasping onto His righteousness and receiving it as our own (2 Cor. 5:22). Then, we must not let go. We need to continue to hold on to the truth of what Jesus did in us. He saved us and made us righteous in His sight by His blood, and He continues to do so no matter what comes up against us.

We are created to be overcomers, triumphing over adversity, laying aside besetting sins, holding fast to our integrity, resisting temptations, and not giving in to the false accusations of our brothers or even the devil. These troubles will not destroy us; they will temper us like steel and refine us like gold. If we do these things, then like Job, we will be able to say, "My heart does not reproach me any of my days." We can approach God with a clean conscience and hands made clean by the blood of Jesus, and we can be assured that He will not reproach us either. Then we can truly approach God boldly and with assurance, knowing that we have the righteousness of His beloved Son and that He will help us to get through whatever we experience in this life, empowered by His grace.

> Let us therefore come boldly unto the throne of
> grace, that we may obtain mercy, and find grace
> to help in time of need. (Heb. 4:16 KJV)

No amount of trouble in this life is greater than the overwhelming power of the grace of God. We are saved by grace, made alive again by grace, and given the power to overcome all the works of the enemy by the grace of God, which resides in us through the Holy Spirit.

NUGGET #9

God's Pleasure

I am young in years and you are old;
Therefore I was shy and afraid to tell you what I think.
"I thought age should speak,
And increased years should teach wisdom.
"But it is a spirit in man,
And the breath of the Almighty gives them understanding.
"The abundant in years may not be wise,
Nor may elders understand justice.
"So I say, 'Listen to me,
I too will tell what I think.'" (Job 32:6–10)

While Job and his three friends argued, there was another man
standing by, waiting his turn to speak. Elihu was younger than Job
or his other friends, and so he had let them have their opportunity
to speak first, hoping that their years would bring wisdom to Job's
predicament. He allowed Job to rant at God, and he allowed the
others to make their accusations about Job's character. This was
as it should be. Respect for one's elders, parents and leaders is a

vital principle of God's kingdom. We do this not because it helps those who are being shown respect, but because it brings life and power to our own selves.

> HONOR YOUR FATHER AND MOTHER (which is the first commandment with a promise), SO THAT IT MAY BE WELL WITH YOU, AND THAT YOU MAY LIVE LONG ON THE EARTH. (Eph. 6:2–3 NASU)

This and other verses make it very clear that the proper order is to show honor to those who are older and more experienced, and to respect the elders and revere their wisdom, which was often gained by making mistakes and then learning to recover from them. The law of Moses equates this with the fear of God.

> You shall rise up before the gray headed and honor the aged, and you shall revere your God; I am the Lord. (Lev. 19:32)

Elihu's statement makes it clear that he expected wisdom to come from those who were senior to him. He waited until they had finished their speeches and allowed Job to finish his justification of himself. He had words to say, but first he allowed his elders to receive their due respect. Then he spoke, but first he needed to clarify something.

"But it is a spirit in man,

And the breath of the Almighty gives them
understanding.
"The abundant in years may not be wise,
Nor may elders understand justice. (Job 32:8–9)

Elihu is making a point here. He has shown respect to his
elders as he should, but he is also saying that the source of wisdom
is not years but the Spirit of God. Wisdom should be expected of
the mature, but it is not limited to the older people because the
source of wisdom, the Holy Spirit, is not limited to any one age
group, gender, denomination, or ethnicity. He can work through
anyone of any age or station if they will only allow themselves to
be His instruments. He speaks through learned scholars, rough
fishermen, shepherd boys, and kings. He is no respecter of persons
or socioeconomic positions. He simply seeks those who will be
obedient and follow His leading. As Elihu so eloquently said, "It
is the Spirit in a man," breathed by the Almighty Himself, that
brings wisdom and understanding.

The same Paul who told the Ephesians to honor their elders
told Timothy not to let others despise him because of his youth.

Let no one look down on your youthfulness, but
rather in speech, conduct, love, faith and purity,
show yourself an example of those who believe.
(1 Tim. 4:12)

These are not contradictory teachings; they are both correct.
Honoring the elder doesn't require showing a lack of respect for
the younger. Both are to be honored because both the young and

the old are the dwelling of the Spirit of God. Elihu could speak wisdom, and so could Job. This teaching about the "Spirit in a man" is for both the old and the young. Many older people are convinced that their usefulness in the kingdom is over. Likewise, many younger people feel that they are not able to be used of God because they are too young. God used the eighty-plus Anna to herald the arrival of the Messiah, and he used the teenaged shepherd boy to defeat the giant. He allowed eighty-five-year-old Caleb to take a mountain that had been waiting for him for forty-five years, and he used a young boy's lunch to feed a multitude. The common factor in all of these is the element of faith and obedience. God wants people of all ages and walks of life in His kingdom active and speaking in faith. This is what Elihu has to teach us.

Elihu's feeling about this is familiar to those who are filled with the Holy Spirit. When He gives us a message for ourselves or someone else, it fills our hearts with elation. We sense an anointing from God, and we want to respond to it. We can't wait to speak. Then the enemy comes in and starts to give us excuses. He says to us, "Who are you that you should speak? This person is older, more educated, more eloquent. Let him speak." Fear rises up and says, "What if this person rejects my word, mocks me, laughs in my face? Why step out and risk the embarrassment of being wrong?"

We try to hide our light under a bushel, saying, "I'm too young, too old, too this, too that." However, we cannot contain the words of God. We know when God wants us to step out in faith and do something outside our comfort zone, but we try to refuse and find ourselves miserable. We flee like Jonah and try to avoid God's leading, but there is no place where He cannot reach us. We finally give in and say, "Okay, Lord, have your way. I will speak, and this frustration will be done." If we go through this enough, we eventually learn to obey His voice early on and avoid the frustration entirely.

Several years ago, I attended a retreat with the men from our small, non-denominational church. My usual reaction to this type of meeting was, "Why do I have to go away to meet with God? Can't he talk to me at my own home, in my own church?" I couldn't come up with a good excuse to not go, however. I went along, sat through the meetings, and enjoyed the fellowship of my brothers, but I continued feeling no closer or further from God than I did at home. It wasn't really a waste of time, but it seemed I could have accomplished as much without leaving my easy chair.

Then on the final day of the retreat, we all gathered for prayer. After joining hands, we formed a circle and prayed. I remember little of what was said that day, but a few things are still crystal clear in my memory. I felt a little nudge from the Spirit to step out of the circle and begin walking around the circle of men. As I walked, we continued to pray. No one seemed to notice, and I was happy with that. I was happy being unobtrusive.

A few laps in, the Spirit reminded me of how the Israelites had walked around Jericho seven times. I realized that I too was instructed to walk around the group seven times. What I didn't understand yet was that the Spirit was tearing down walls in me. After I finished my seventh lap, I quietly rejoined the group, and we continued praying.

The Bible teaches that if we are faithful in small things, we will be trusted with even more. The Spirit of God was not done with me. Because I responded to his call to do a small thing, He could lead me out into something even deeper. I heard His voice tell me to pray for someone's neck. This was going to take a much bigger step out in faith. I debated within myself. "If I speak out and there is no one whose neck is hurting, I'll be embarrassed. Why don't you use one of the official members of the staff?" But His call was clear. "You need to pray for someone's sore neck." Finally I relented and spoke up. "Is there someone here who has a sore neck? I would like to pray for you."

One of the elders of the church spoke up immediately, "My neck is sore. This is for me." As I prayed and laid hands on him, the power of God almost knocked us down in opposite directions. His neck was immediately relieved. The next few minutes became a blur. Many more men asked me to pray for them. I never knew that our little church had so many pains in the neck! Many years later, I still remember driving myself home and not fully understanding what had happened. I asked the Lord why he chose to use me that day and on many other days since. His answer was simple and direct because that is how I relate to others. He said, "Because you will." In spite of my lack of formal education, my bluntness, and my lack of a title within the church—or maybe because of these things—He can use me. But mostly it is because I am willing to do what He says, even if it is a little foolish or might bring me embarrassment.

I was fortunate in that I was part of a fellowship that encouraged laypeople to serve wherever they could, and so I was able to continue listening and obeying the Lord's leading. He has spoken to me many times since. Every time, the same argument plays out in my head. "Lord, isn't there someone else? What if no one responds? What if I'm wrong?" There have been times when I wanted to step back, warm up my piece of pew, and let someone else pick up the mantle. I have learned that I can't live with the dissatisfaction of knowing that I missed out on a blessing from God—and worse yet, so did someone else.

This brings up another aspect that comes into play: the sovereignty of God. If I choose not to act on what the Spirit is asking me to do, then He will often use someone else who is willing to do His bidding. By refusing, I cannot stand in the way of what the eternal God wants to accomplish. The only thing that I can do is deny myself any opportunity to experience the blessing that comes with being obedient to Christ. Thinking in this manner keeps me humble in the knowledge that I am not irreplaceable. Another facet of this gem of the sovereignty of God is that if I make a mistake, don't hear correctly, or even out and out disobey, there is nothing that I am capable of messing up to the point that the Almighty can't fix it.

It is not because I am the oldest, youngest, wisest, strongest, and smartest, and it's definitely not because I have the most letters behind my name. It is because He chose me, and the reason He chose me is because I would do what He asked. It is impossible for me to not speak what the Lord has placed in me. I know that is a double negative, but it's the best way to express how I feel about this. I have a choice to obey or not, but it is really not a choice at all. When He calls, I must listen and obey.

It was the same for Elihu. The Spirit of God was working mightily in Elihu. He must have been barely able to contain himself.

> "For I am full of words;
> The spirit within me constrains me.
> "Behold, my belly is like unvented wine,
> Like new wineskins it is about to burst." (Job 32:18–19)

His words were ready to burst out of him like a shaken soda can. He was working to contain his own spirit, which was begging for relief.

> "Let me speak that I may get relief;
> Let me open my lips and answer." (Job 32:20)

He had to speak what was in him, or he would explode. He had waited for his elders, respected their position, and given them the respect they were due. Now it was his turn.

Elihu addresses Job's complaint.

> "Surely you have spoken in my hearing,
> And I have heard the sound of your words:
> 'I am pure, without transgression;
> I am innocent and there is no guilt in me.
> 'Behold, He invents pretexts against me;
> He counts me as His enemy.
> 'He puts my feet in the stocks;

He watches all my paths.'" (Job 33:8–11)

Job has proclaimed his purity and perfection throughout while at the same time accusing God of an injustice. This is not a sin; otherwise when the story is summed up later, God could not say that "in all this Job did not sin." This is a lack of understanding of the ways and nature of God. Elihu is quick to point this out.

"Behold, let me tell you, you are not right in this,
for God is greater than man." (Job 33:12)

Elihu has been waiting his turn long enough. When he gets going, he cannot stop. His sermon goes on for five chapters. He tells Job that God is not unjust, but that God is higher than Job and Elihu and us. His ways are not our ways, and if we try to fit Him into that box, He will not go. Elihu proclaims the goodness and rightness of God, and he says that God's allowing of trouble in our lives is not because he is unjust, but because He has something that He wants to work out in our lives, and it will work out for our ultimate good. He allows trouble to come so that He can root out pride in our lives and deliver us from the ravages of death.

"Behold, God does all these oftentimes with men,
To bring back his soul from the pit,
That he may be enlightened with the light of life."
(Job 33:29–30)

Job's problem here is that he is trying to relate to God as he would a man, but God is not a man. He is greater than men, and

His ways are higher than our ways. Elihu eloquently points this out to Job.

> "Surely, God will not act wickedly,
> And the Almighty will not pervert justice.
> "Who gave Him authority over the earth?
> And who has laid on Him the whole world?
> "If He should determine to do so,
> If He should gather to Himself His spirit and
> His breath,
> All flesh would perish together,
> And man would return to dust." (Job 34:12–15)

God cannot be unjust because He is the one who defines justice. No man—not Job, not Elihu, not you, and not I—gave the Almighty His authority. He is in a place of authority because He is the creator of heaven and earth and the giver of life. If He took back His breath, life would cease to exist. If He wants to test us and try us in the refiner's fire, that is true to His nature and consistent with His justice.

When Job complained that God was treating him unfairly, he was really saying that he was more righteous than God. Elihu points this out to Job and his friends and then asks them an interesting question. Does it take anything away from God when we sin? Does it add anything to God when we are righteous?

> "Do you think this is according to justice?
> Do you say, 'My righteousness is more than
> God's'?

"For you say, 'What advantage will it be to You?
What profit will I have, more than if I had sinned?'
"I will answer you,
And your friends with you.
"Look at the heavens and see;
And behold the clouds—they are higher than you.
"If you have sinned, what do you accomplish
against Him?
And if your transgressions are many, what do you
do to Him?
"If you are righteous, what do you give to Him,
Or what does He receive from your hand?
"Your wickedness is for a man like yourself,
And your righteousness is for a son of man. (Job
35:2–8)

God doesn't need us to be righteous. He very much desires
that we be righteous, but if we sin, it doesn't take away anything
that makes Him who He is. Our sin doesn't take away from
His righteousness. It does not damage Him, but it damages us.
However, He is pleased by our righteous obedience and our sincere
yearning for His pleasure in us.

Many of us never experience this pleasure of God. It's not
because we are displeasing to Him, but because we mistakenly
believe that He is naturally displeased with the world in general
and with us and our actions in particular. We understand on an
intellectual level from the scriptures that he is not pleased by the
offerings of bulls and goats, but by obedience to His commands

(1 Sam. 15:22; Isa. 1:11). But somehow we never get to a place where we can think of Him as being pleased with us. We see our own weaknesses and failings, and we think that a holy God could never be pleased with us. We think the best we can hope for is to deflect His wrath. And when we experience trouble, we think that it is because He is displeased with us. This is not what His word says, though.

> For I delight in loyalty rather than sacrifice,
> And in the knowledge of God rather than burnt
> offerings. (Hosea 6:6)

He says here that He delights in our knowledge of Him! He doesn't want the blood of bulls. The root of the word that is translated as *knowledge* here is used elsewhere in the Old Testament to describe the relations between husbands and wives. It denotes an intimate relationship between two willing souls. He wants us to experience His pleasure in us as we experience intimacy with the living God. This is difficult for some of us to accept, though. We don't think He could possibly be pleased with us, but we are wrong.

When we accept and acknowledge Jesus as our savior and Lord, we are said to put on Christ. In other words, we are clothed in who Jesus Christ is.

> And all who have been united with Christ in
> baptism have put on the character of Christ, like
> putting on new clothes. (Gal. 3:27 NLT)

When we put on Christ, our relationship with the Father is the same as the relationship that Jesus has with the Father. What is the nature of this relationship?

> After being baptized, Jesus came up immediately from the water; and behold, the heavens were opened, and he saw the Spirit of God descending as a dove and lighting on Him, and behold, a voice out of the heavens said, "This is My beloved Son, *in whom I am well-pleased.*" (Matt. 3:16–17 my emphasis)

This is hard for some of us to accept, but it is biblical truth. If you are a believer, united in baptism with Christ, then God is pleased with you. If you are experiencing trouble, it is not because God has abandoned you or is displeased with you. It is because God has a greater purpose in mind for you. He wants to use your life and experience of Him to bring greater glory to Himself. He also wants to allow you to experience pleasure in your knowledge of Him, as well as to experience His pleasure in you. This was the purpose of all the trouble that was allowed in Job's life. This was the thing that Job's learned friends didn't understand, but that young Elihu stated most eloquently. Even he and Job and Hosea only saw this from afar on the other side of the cross. As they looked forward to the Father's pleasure in His Son, they experienced the shadows of the intimacy with God that was to come. We look backward to the cross as we put on Christ Jesus and experience God's pleasure in our obedience to Him. In Christ Jesus, we are pleasing to God, and we can experience

His pleasure in us. This does not produce pride in us because we know that it is only through the shed blood of Jesus that this is so. Instead, we realize that to deny God's pleasure in us and to not take pleasure in Him is to devalue the blood that Jesus shed to seal that relationship.

God is pleased with us!

NUGGET #10

Speaking God's Word

"For I am full of words;
The spirit within me constrains me.
"Behold, my belly is like unvented wine,
Like new wineskins it is about to burst." (Job 32:18–19)

Elihu is continuing to speak here. He is not saying that he has an upset stomach, though. The youngest member of the group is saying that the Spirit of the Lord has given him something to say. When God calls someone to speak a word on His behalf into someone else's life, the urge to speak can sometimes be almost irresistible. But Elihu has been exercising self-control, allowing his elders to speak first and deferring to their positions as leaders in the land. He politely waited his turn, but now he can wait no longer. He must speak what God has given him. The next six chapters record Elihu's powerful, prophetic message. He chastises Job for his grumbling accusations of unfairness on God's part, and he delivers a powerful affirmation of God's goodness and awesome power. Sprinkled throughout this message, we find a very clear and concise message about the function of the prophet and the administration of the prophetic gift.

The prophetic gift and the office of the prophet are among the most misunderstood and misused functions of the church today. The beliefs and opinions on this subject vary widely from denomination to denomination and from congregation to congregation. Some insist that the office of prophet and the gift of prophecy are no longer valid. Others believe that these are the foremost part of church life.

To those who subscribe to the former camp, I realize that you base much of your objection to this activity on the words of Paul from 1 Corinthians 13:8, "but if there are gifts of prophecy, they will be done away." At no point does Paul give a date for when this would happen, and even if he did, the rest of the verse would apply to seeking of spiritual knowledge also, because this is linked to the same primary clause in his statement. No one believes that Paul advocates ceasing to seek knowledge of God. His point in this is not that prophecy would soon pass away, but that the most important and lasting feature of Christian life is not prophecy or tongues or even seeking knowledge of God, but love. He devotes the entire next chapter of his epistle to teaching the proper administration of these vocal gifts, but he first had to establish that the primary motivation of all Christian life is to be love, both for Christ and our fellow man.

To those who subscribe to the latter view, I feel that I must point out that Paul was very clear. These gifts are to be used in a proper and orderly manner, and above all else, they are to be practiced with love for Christ and love for our neighbors. These are the greatest and second greatest commands, and no amount of anointing and calling of God supersedes this. The fivefold ministry of apostles, prophets, evangelists, pastors, and teachers (Eph. 4:11–12) does not set one of these above the other. On the contrary, the Scriptures are clear that each of the various gifts is in need of the others (1 Cor. 12:20), and that all these gifts are secondary to love (1 Cor. 13:1, 8, 13). Paul encouraged the believers at Corinth to seek these spiritual gifts, and he urged them to use them properly.

The fact is that God uses people to deliver His message both publicly and privately, sometimes to large groups and sometimes to individuals. This is the gift of prophecy and the office of the prophet. The gift of prophecy has been used and misused since the days of the apostles. People have done foolish things and suffered irreparable harm at the urging of people who claim to be prophets, and some people have experienced the blessing of God because they heeded the words of God's prophets speaking into their lives. The problem is that at the end of the day, prophets are still human. They are subject to the same weaknesses that afflict all mankind. They don't always understand clearly, they sometimes don't speak clearly, and when they get it right, they are subject to be overtaken with pride just like the rest of us. Often the problem lies with the hearer not hearing the message as God intended, or not testing a word against the scriptures to assess its validity. Sometimes a prophet can allow people to put him upon a pedestal of honor that should be reserved for God alone. Much scripture has been devoted to the proper administration of this gift. This brings us back to Elihu.

"For I am full of words;
The spirit within me constrains me.
"Behold, my belly is like unvented wine,
Like new wineskins it is about to burst." (Job
32:18–19)

Elihu has a message from God for Job, and it is threatening to explode him from within if he doesn't release the word that God has placed in him. He has a word for Job, but he also can teach us how to approach this subject when we believe that God wants to use us in this area. He can also teach us how to receive a word from God through another believer.

The most important thing to remember is that the word from God must come from God. It does not originate from the prophet. It does not belong to the prophet. It is God's word. It is the most powerful thing in the universe because at the word of God, the universe came into being. It has the power to build, to tear down, to wound, and to heal; the power of life and death are in His word (Heb. 11:3; Ps. 107:20; Isa. 24:33; Ezek. 37:4). His word brings life to our spirits.

> "It is the Spirit who gives life; the flesh profits nothing; the *words that I have spoken to you are spirit and are life.*" (John 6:63; my emphasis)

The word translated here as *words* is once again *rhema*. *Vine's Expository Dictionary of Biblical Words* defines this word as "that which is spoken, what is uttered in speech or writing." It is a word or a statement that someone makes. In this case, Jesus says that the words he spoke from the Father are capable of bringing life to our spirits. This word (*rhema*) is different from the Word (*logos*) of John chapter 1. The *logos* is the living embodiment of the mind or thought of God expressed in the man Jesus. The *rhema* is a spoken word that can be wielded as a sword to defeat the enemy (Eph. 6:17) and bring faith, which leads to eternal salvation (Rom. 10:17).

Elihu acknowledges that the word he has comes from the spirit within him. In Job 36:2, he says he is speaking on God's behalf. In verse 3 he says he receives his wisdom from "afar off, from of old." In Job 33:4 he acknowledges God as the source of his message. He does not claim these words as his own but as a message from God. God has placed this message in his heart, and it is going to burst out if he doesn't let it out in a proper manner.

When one has a *rhema* word from God, it makes the heart leap with joy and can cause some consternation. We ask ourselves, "Is this really from God, or is it just me?" At the same time, a piece of our hearts knows that what we have heard is a message from God. God always seems to leave some room for doubt in this area. I believe He does this so that we have room for our faith to be active. If there is no room for doubt, there is no room for us to step out in faith.

A wonderful picture of this at work is in the popular motion picture *Indiana Jones and the Last Crusade*. Near the end of the story, Dr. Indiana Jones is posed with a dilemma called the leap of faith. He needs to cross a seemingly bottomless chasm to achieve his goal. To cross, he must step out onto nothingness, risking his life and the life of his dying father. He takes a step forward, and just a little down, and amazingly there is an invisible bridge that supports his weight and allows him to cross. Once he crosses, he throws sand on the bridge, and those behind him can see it in order to cross.

Dr. Jones has stepped out in faith because the possibility of destruction is there for him. The others who follow are not exercising a leap of faith because they can see, and there is no room for doubt.

The principle here is that sometimes we must take a step to find out whether what we believe is true. The risk—being dashed to pieces on rocks—may not be the same, but for some of us, the prospect of humiliation is worse. We know we have a message, but we risk that it may not be well received, it may be misunderstood, or it may be rejected outright. It might even garner us criticism and censure by those in authority.

Despite all these possibilities, the message is there, trying to make its way out, very nearly bursting us at our seams. We know to sit on our hands and do nothing is to miss out on what God wants to do in and through us. We find ourselves facing an invisible bridge over a chasm of humiliation and rejection. On the other side, unreachable by any other means, is the peace in our spirit that comes from knowing we have obeyed God fully. We know in our spirit that the word we have is from God, but the only way to know that this is true is to take that leap of faith, risk looking foolish, and do what we believe God is asking of us.

This is where Elihu finds himself. He has a message to bring. It is pressuring him from the inside, but he is the youngest of the group. He waits his turn. He allows his elders to say their piece. Then he takes a step.

"Let me speak that I may get relief;
Let me open my lips and answer." (Job 32:20)

Elihu begins his speech with a caveat. He is not going to show any partiality or favoritism. He is not going to flatter Job or anyone else. To do so would be to provoke the Almighty. He has to tell it like it is.

"Let me now be partial to no one,
Nor flatter any man.
"For I do not know how to flatter,
Else my Maker would soon take me away." (Job 32:21–22)

When we receive a word from God, it has the power of life and death. It can build someone up or tear them down. Whether it has a negative or positive effect is sometimes dependent on the way that we deliver the word, or on the way the heart of the hearer receives it. If we speak with harshness, we can wound irreparably. If we speak too softly, sugar-coating our words, we can dilute the message. If we show partiality in our words in order to curry favor with those in authority, we lose the message entirely.

In the days of the kings of Israel, there were many prophets. King Ahab called on his prophets and seers to help him rule his kingdom. Many of these were not true prophets but flatterers who told Ahab what they believed he wanted to hear (1 Kings 22:5–23). Because of this, it was easy for the Lord to send a spirit to deceive them and Ahab in order to bring about his destruction.

There was another prophet in the land who spoke the word of God. His name was Micaiah. At the insistence of the righteous king of Judah, Jehoshaphat, Ahab consulted this prophet, although Ahab noted, "He never says anything good about me" (1 Kings 22:8). This was probably because there was very little good to be said about Ahab. Micaiah was called before Ahab, and he spoke the truth (1 Kings 22:17–23) He warned Ahab of the coming destruction. He spoke boldly and told Ahab that if Ahab survived the coming battle, then Micaiah was no prophet. As gamblers say, Micaiah was all in. Micaiah spoke the truth, and Ahab was destroyed as predicted. Micaiah didn't flatter or show partiality. He simply delivered the word God had given him.

Sometimes God calls us to be bold like Micaiah. Sometimes He desires a different approach. King David had sinned egregiously when he took Bathsheba to his bed and then plotted to have her husband killed to cover up his sin (2 Sam. 11). In order to bring David to a place of repentance, a different approach was required. The Lord sent His word to his prophet Nathan. Nathan went before the king and led with a parable (2 Sam. 12:1–4). He used the parable of a stolen sheep to get under David's hardness of heart. David was a shepherd at heart and understood the care of shepherds for their sheep. This soft approach allowed Nathan to get inside David's defenses and bring the rebuke that God had sent him to give David (2 Sam. 12:7–15). Nathan didn't hold back the message; he didn't flatter or show partiality to David. Under the direction of the Spirit of God, he softened the message just enough to get it into David's heart, and David received it.

This is how Elihu approaches his message to Job and his friends.

At times he is bold, challenging Job to refute him if possible (Job 33:5). At other times, he speaks softly and prays that God will deliver Job from his troubles (Job 33:23–28). He tells Job to listen carefully and promises that Job will have a chance to respond to his words. Above all, he speaks the truth to Job. Like the later prophets, he speaks boldly to one who is his societal superior without showing any partiality. To put this in New Testament terms, Elihu is "no respecter of persons." He doesn't honor someone who is socially or economically greater than he simply because of the man's status. He honors Job for who he is: a child of God.

> "Behold, I belong to God like you;
> I too have been formed out of the clay." (Job 33:6)

The apostle James encourages this same impartiality. (James 2:1–9) We should not show favoritism in our words or actions with the hope of receiving some favor or improving our own standing in the community. We should honor people in the church as who they are, fellow believers, children of God, and joint heirs with Christ. We should speak the truth softly to some and firmly to others. This is not showing partiality but awareness of the different needs of different individuals. Micaiah, Nathan, and Elihu didn't show partiality, but they all spoke differently.

> "My words are from the uprightness of my heart,
> And my lips speak knowledge sincerely.
> "The Spirit of God has made me,
> And the breath of the Almighty gives me life."
> (Job 33:3–4)

Elihu then names the source of his message. In verse 4 he says that the breath of the Almighty has inspired the message. The Spirit of God has made Elihu, and God Himself has breathed the message into Elihu. But there is something else at work here. That other factor in this equation is Elihu's own sincerity and uprightness of heart. Elihu says, "The uprightness of my heart."

What happens when a prophet lacks this quality is demonstrated in another Old Testament prophet, Balaam of Beor. Balaam was recognized as a prophet for hire. He sold his gift to the highest bidder, and in this case the high bidder was Balak, the king of Moab. Balak feared that the Israelites would take away his kingdom, and so he tried to hire Balaam to pronounce a curse from God onto the Israelites (Num. 22:1–6).

Balaam told Balak's representatives that he could not curse the Israelites because God had blessed them. (Num. 22:7–14). Balak wouldn't take no for an answer, though. He sent more distinguished representatives and offered more money to Balaam. Balaam agreed to go with him but still was prevented from cursing the Israelites. Instead, he pronounced three blessings on Israel (Num. 23–24). But still, he wanted Balak's money, and so he devised a plan. He showed the Moabites how to entice the Israelites to sin with the women of Moab, and he taught the Moabites to draw the Israelites into their idolatry so the Israelites would bring destruction on themselves (Num. 25:1–9; Num. 31:16). Balaam had the gift of the prophet, but he didn't have the uprightness of heart that a true prophet requires. His heart was divided. He said, "I can only say what God tells me to say." This statement is an accurate representation of the office of prophet, and if Balaam had stopped there, his name would have gone down with the list of the righteous prophets. Balaam wanted money and the honor of men, though. As a result, he was destroyed when the Israelites slaughtered the Moabites. His lack of uprightness of heart led to the destruction of twenty-four thousand Israelites, the majority of the Moabite race, and Balaam himself. Without a noble, upright character, a prophet is nothing.

Paul wrote of this to the Corinthians.

> If I have the gift of prophecy, and know all mysteries and all knowledge; and if I have all faith, so as to remove mountains, but do not have love, I am nothing.
> (1 Cor. 13:2)

It is not enough to simply hear and speak the word of God. The prophet must do so in love, loving God above all and loving others as himself. This is the greatest commandment, and no gift of prophecy can supersede this command. The prophet must desire to edify or build up the body of Christ.

> But one who prophesies speaks to men for edification and exhortation and consolation. One who speaks in a tongue edifies himself; but one who prophesies edifies the church. Now I wish that you all spoke in tongues, but even more that you would prophesy; and greater is one who prophesies than one who speaks in tongues,

unless he interprets, so that the church may receive edifying.
(1 Cor. 14:3–5)

Paul says the prophet, speaking in love, should edify, exhort, and console. Edification is the process of building up something. This is the desire of the prophet: to see the church built up not just in numbers, but by strengthening the faith and knowledge of God in its members. The prophet exhorts the people both individually and as a group to press in further and become closer to God and what He is doing in His people. The prophet also consoles those who are experiencing trouble with the comfort that is to be found in the word of God.

This is what Elihu was doing. He was encouraging Job to seek and find what God was doing in his life, giving him comfort in his time of trouble. Where others had sought to tear Job down, Elihu was seeking to lift Job up toward the Lord and His ways.

> "Behold, I belong to God like you; I too have been formed out of the clay.
> "Behold, no fear of me should terrify you, nor should my pressure weigh heavily on you." (Job 33:6–7)

Elihu is speaking from a place of humility. He didn't say, "Listen to my words, for God has spoken to me and not to you." He acknowledges his humanity: "I too have been formed out of the clay." Finding the balance point between the humility of recognizing the humanity of the prophet and the divine nature of the word of God that the prophet brings is tricky. The word of God is a mighty thing, dividing between soul and spirit, tearing down strongholds, setting captives free, healing the sick, and opening the eyes of the blind. But the Lord has chosen to bring this word to the world through people who are made from dirt. The Lord takes that dirt, speaks His words over it, and breathes life into it—and it becomes something mighty. Yes, His word is mighty in and through us, but we must remember above all else, we are all made from the same stuff. The only difference is that at times His Spirit sets us apart for the work which He has chosen for us. We balance the weight of the power of the word of God against our humanity. We don't fear the prophet, and neither do we disdain him. We don't fear the word of God in our lives, and we don't fear the one who brings it. He is human, made from the same dirt as us, and as such he is sometimes subject to the same weaknesses and empowered by the same Spirit. The recognition of this fact should keep the prophet humble and, through that humility of spirit, capable of being used of God.

It would be much easier if God spoke to His people with a booming voice from heaven, but that is not the way He has chosen to do things. He speaks through His written word and through his people, whom He formed from clay. He speaks to us in the still, small voice in the middle of the night, and He speaks to us through the person sitting next to us on the pew. Sometimes we don't get the message right. Sometimes we don't hear what the *rhema* word of God has to say to us. Sometimes our humanity gets in the way of the message. But He has a way of seeing that His message gets through in spite of the earthen vessels He has chosen to use. The thing to remember in all of this is that the message is His, and it is more important and more powerful than the vessel that carries it.

This takes the weight of responsibility off the one who is delivering the message. If the message is not ours, it is not our responsibility to make it come to pass. It is not our responsibility to put pressure on someone else and make him act upon it. Elihu said, "Nor should my pressure weigh heavily on you." Elihu's words are not heavy. He doesn't demand that Job obey him. He simply reveals what God has shown him and allows Job to respond to God.

His words are firm, though. He quotes Job's complaints that he has been treated unfairly by God, and then he tells Job the truth.

> "Behold, let me tell you, you are not right in this,
> for God is greater than man.
> "Why do you complain against Him That He
> does not give an account of all His doings?" (Job
> 33:12–13)

Job's complaint was that God was not being held to account for His actions. He was demanding an explanation of the actions of a sovereign God. God is not required to explain Himself to us or justify His actions. He is God. He doesn't have to explain His actions to us, but He does. Let's read on.

> "Indeed God speaks once,
> Or twice, yet no one notices it.
> In a dream, a vision of the night,

When sound sleep falls on men,
While they slumber in their beds,
Then He opens the ears of men,
And seals their instruction,
That He may turn man aside from his conduct,
And keep man from pride;
He keeps back his soul from the pit,
And his life from passing over into Sheol." (Job 33:14–18)

When we are in the middle of trouble, it is often difficult to hear God, but He is still speaking to us. He speaks in the stillness of the night with the still, small voice. Like Elijah, we are looking for the earthquake and the thunder, but when He speaks in the little things, we can often miss it. He uses others to speak encouragement to our hopelessness. He uses the little things to speak to us to keep us from pride.

But He gives a greater grace. Therefore it says, "GOD IS OPPOSED TO THE PROUD, BUT GIVES GRACE TO THE HUMBLE." Submit therefore to God. Resist the devil and he will flee from you. (James 4:6–7)

A humble spirit is submitted to the sovereignty of God and His will. This humble, submitted spirit is powerful and capable of resisting and overcoming the devil and all his plans and purposes.

Then Elihu continued and said,
"Hear my words, you wise men, and listen to me,
you who know.
"For the ear tests words as the palate tastes food.
"Let us choose for ourselves what is right; Let
us know among ourselves what is good." (Job
34:1–4)

The words of the prophet must be tested. Here, Elihu is speaking to the whole group. He calls them wise men and "you who know." He honors his hearers, but he also gives them a responsibility. They are required to test his words. This statement provokes more questions than answers. How does this process work? Who are these wise men whose ears are to test the word? How are they to do this testing? What are the criteria that they use to test the word?

First let us deal with the who. Elihu is speaking here to the whole group that has come to comfort Job. He is also speaking to Job, and in verse 4 he includes himself, saying, "Let us know among ourselves." Everyone present has a responsibility to test the word that Elihu is speaking. This principle is born out in the New Testament too. Paul devoted most of the fourteenth chapter of his first letter to the Corinthian church to the proper administration of spiritual gifts such as prophecy.

Let two or three prophets speak, and let the
others pass judgment. But if a revelation is made
to another who is seated, the first one must keep
silent. For you can all prophesy one by one, so

that all may learn and all may be exhorted; and
the spirits of prophets are subject to prophets; for
God is not a God of confusion but of peace, as in
all the churches of the saints. (1 Cor. 14:29–33)

John also deals with how the gifts are to be received.

Beloved, do not believe every spirit, but test the
spirits to see whether they are from God, because
many false prophets have gone out into the world.
(1 John 4:1)

Paul says that we are to pass judgment. John says to test the
spirits. Both of them are telling us the same thing. Elihu says the
ear tastes the words as the palate tastes food. On the surface, this
seems absurd. The tongue is the organ of taste. The ear is for
hearing. How does the ear taste words? It doesn't really; Elihu is
using a metaphor here. He is creating a picture of a food taster in
an early royal court.

Many of the ancient rulers had people in their court who were
designated as food tasters, to protect the king from poisoning.
They would sample the king's food before he ate to make sure
that there was no poison in it. This is the image that Elihu's word
evokes in the mind. This protected both the king and the cook. If
the cook knew that the king's food would be tasted beforehand,
there was no sense in trying to poison the food. What assassin
wants to risk the gallows to kill a lackey? Like the food taster, we
are to sample the words of the prophet and put them to the taste
test. We listen to the words of a prophet, and we judge them as to

whether or not they ring true in our hearts with the Spirit of God who dwells in each of us. We test them against the written word of God. The written word of God is the final arbiter of whether or not the words spoken by a prophet are true.

This principle honors both the prophet and the hearer. Notice that Elihu calls his hearers wise men and men of knowledge. We are not minor, expendable members of the king's court. We are children of the king endowed with a responsibility to the kingdom. We are not to simply take the words of anyone who claims to be a prophet and swallow them whole. Instead, we are to taste and test the words of the prophet, comparing them to the written word of God and to the living Word of God who dwells in us.

> If a prophet or a dreamer of dreams arises among you and gives you a sign or a wonder, and the sign or the wonder comes true, concerning which he spoke to you, saying, 'Let us go after other gods (whom you have not known) and let us serve them,' you shall not listen to the words of that prophet or that dreamer of dreams; for the Lord your God is testing you to find out if you love the Lord your God with all your heart and with all your soul. (Deut. 13:1–3)

This part is very simple. If a prophet tells us to do something that is clearly against the Word of God, like committing adultery, we should not heed his word. In the Old Testament, that prophet would have been executed. We can only ask him to recant his words, to repent of his behavior, and to be reconciled to God. We can order him to be quiet, to stop preaching heresy, and to submit to the leadership of the church. Finally, we can put him out of the fellowship if he persists.

Once the criteria of the written word have been met, though, we still have a further obligation. Suppose someone says to you, "The Lord has spoken to me that you are supposed to be involved in this ministry or that program in the church." These are not sinful things, but they may or may not be the direction that God has for your life right now. How do we judge this word?

Elihu gives us a test that we can use to discern the accuracy of the words of the prophet. It comes back to the taste test. How do the words of the prophet taste? Do they have the ring of truth? Do they confirm something that you already felt and believed in your heart? Very often, the words of a prophet will confirm what the hearer already knew deep within his heart. Does the word cause your heart to leap with excitement, or is there no passion aroused by them? This doesn't mean that a little bit of fear doesn't rise up; that is normal when one is asked to step out in faith. Ananias must have had a little bit of fear when the Lord spoke to him and told him to baptize the murderous Saul, who had come to send the brothers to prison. But Ananias knew that the word he had received was from the Lord. Ananias was obedient and went to baptize Saul as he was ordered, at the risk of his life. Without his obedience today, half the New Testament would be missing, or someone else would be acknowledged as the one who baptized Paul. But today we recognize Ananias as a man of faith. A little bit of fear is a healthy thing. Stepping out in spite of fear produces eternal results.

"Wait for me a little, and I will show you
That there is yet more to be said in God's behalf.
"I will fetch my knowledge from afar,
And I will ascribe righteousness to my Maker."
(Job 36:2–3)

Elihu has more to say. He makes it clear here that this word from God is meant to do something else. It must bring honor and glory to God. Elihu's words are spoken on God's behalf. He says he wishes to use words that show how righteous and just God is. The entire thirty-sixth chapter is devoted to Elihu's description of God and His attributes.

He describes God as a just judge of mankind. (Job 36:6, 11–12). Elihu depicts God as calling to His people, exposing their sin, and exhorting them to repent, promising blessings would accompany obedience. (Job 36:9–11, 15–16) He describes God as unique and holy, exalted above all else, without peer. (Job 36:22–23) He begins by calling God mighty, and he ends the chapter with a description of God's might as displayed in a storm. (Job 36:5, 27–33) This is the essence of the prophet. He brings honor to God and exalts the God of heaven. This provokes a response of awe on Elihu's part.

"At this also my heart trembles,
And leaps from its place." (Job 37:1)

Elihu is swept up in the greatness of God. He says his heart leaps at the sound of God's voice. This is awe. In our modern speech, we have often misused the word *awesome*. Elihu is describing his feelings as he recognizes God's greatness. His heart trembles and leaps from its place.

Elihu describes the might of God displayed in the power of nature that He has created. He tells how mighty God is by showing His power over the storms. As Elihu begins to speak, a literal storm is brewing, which Elihu uses as an illustration of God's might.

> "After it, a voice roars;
> He thunders with His majestic voice,
> And He does not restrain the lightnings when His
> voice is heard." (Job 37:4)

He attributes the cold of winter and the heat in the summer to God's hand.

> "From the breath of God ice is made,
> And the expanse of the waters is frozen." (Job
> 37:10)

> You whose garments are hot,
> When the land is still because of the south wind?
> (Job 37:17)

Then he asks Job to compare himself to the might of God.

> "Listen to this, O Job,
> Stand and consider the wonders of God.
> "Do you know how God establishes them,
> And makes the lightning of His cloud to shine?

"Do you know about the layers of the thick clouds,

The wonders of one perfect in knowledge,

You whose garments are hot,

When the land is still because of the south wind?

"Can you, with Him, spread out the skies,

Strong as a molten mirror?" (Job 37:14–18)

As we will see in chapter 38, Job is moved to repentance. God is glorified and honored. When Job compares himself to God, he is undone. The purpose of prophecy is not simply to show our frailty, but to reveal God to us. When this happens, the natural result is that we see how small we are in relation to God. However, we also see how mighty He is who cares for us in our insignificance. This in turn raises us up toward Him in worship.

Elihu has reached the end of his speech. He has shown us the essence of the office of the prophet. He has responded humbly to the word that God has given him. He has gently brought correction to Job, his elder and social superior. He has spoken boldly the words that have been given to him. He has asked wise men to test the word given and see whether it is true. He has honored God and lifted Job from the pit of bitterness to the awe of God.

NUGGET #11

Mercy and Goodness

"I have heard of You by the hearing of the ear;
But now my eye sees You;
Therefore I retract,
And I repent in dust and ashes." (Job 42:5–6)

After Elihu finishes his speech, the Lord appears to Job in the middle of the storm. He asks Job the rhetorical question, "Who do you think you are and who do you think I am?" Then He begins to list things that He has done that no man can possibly do. As Job is forced to make the comparison, he logically comes up short.

"Behold, I am insignificant; what can I reply to You?
I lay my hand on my mouth.
"Once I have spoken, and I will not answer;
Even twice, and I will add nothing more." (Job 40:4–5)

"Therefore I retract,
And I repent in dust and ashes." (Job 42:6)

Job is truly filled with repentance for his accusations against God. He knows that he is the creation and that the Lord is his creator. God is ruler of the universe, and Job recognizes that. Nevertheless, Job's life is still filled with trouble. His children are still gone. His wife is still angry. His fortune is still lost. His body is still broken. He has accused God of treating him unfairly and demanded that God answer for His cruelty. There is an old saying, "Be careful what you ask for. You might get it." Job asked for God to answer his charges, and God did. God answered Job's accusations by showing who He is. He is the creator of the universe, and He's Job's creator too. He has the right as ruler of the whole world to do as He wills. Anyone who would take that right from Him must show the ability to do what God has done: create a universe from nothing. If one is able to do this, that one has a right to accuse God of being unjust. Job realized that he could not challenge God on His level, and so he did the best thing he could do. He clapped his hand over his mouth and shut up.

This place of mourning, where Job was, is where many of us find ourselves. We feel that God has rejected us and is tormenting us beyond our ability to endure. We fear that we may never be whole, that our lives will never have meaning, and that our journey is in vain. Like Job, we see the power and holiness of the Almighty, and we hear Him ask, "Who is this who darkens my counsel?" We look at ourselves and compare ourselves to God, and we feel insignificant. We want to retract our accusations that God is unfair and unjust, and we hold our hand over our mouths. But like Job, we are still surrounded by trouble, and we ask, "Why?"

We acknowledge that He is all-powerful, all-knowing, and all-present. If He is all these things, and if He cares about us as He says, then why does He allow the enemy to bring destruction into our lives? Why does the all-powerful God not do something to relieve our miseries? If we could see some purpose in it, we might be able to endure it. This is how I felt many years ago, when I saw everything that mattered to me being assaulted by the enemy. I was frustrated and angry and willing to try anything to get out of the Trouble.

To get out of the trouble—that is where the problem arises. We want out of the trouble, and we want out now. The frustrating part is that deep down, we know that our God is capable of getting us out of our troubles miraculously, immediately, and decisively. He is capable, but sometimes He seems unwilling. He doesn't seem to want to get us out of our trouble. He could have miraculously and instantly delivered Job from his troubles. He could have healed Job's sores, resurrected Job's children, and given him a treasure chest of gold to buy more livestock, but He didn't. He allowed Job to suffer in the ash pit. But to what purpose?

Back to my story for a moment. Unlike Job, who was blameless from the start, I was not blameless. I was arrogant, self-centered, and proud. I had faith in only one thing, really, and that was me and my ability to earn a living. My job and my ability to do my job identified me; it was who I was. Then it was gone. I had no job and no way to provide but to use up what my wife and I had saved. I watched over the weeks and months as the savings dwindled, and I railed like Job, saying, "Why, Lord, why?" I wanted out of the Trouble. I wanted an instantaneous, miraculous solution. I wanted to go back to what I was: provider, wage earner, bringer home of the bacon. God had other plans, though. He didn't want to get me out of the Trouble. He wanted to bring me *through* the Trouble.

This may seem like a fine distinction, but it is very important. The reason He didn't get me out of my Trouble is because He wanted me to see that He would get me through whatever came up. He wanted me to learn these nuggets of truth that we have been discussing, and the only way to do this was to walk me through the Valley of Trouble.

As He walked me through the Valley of Trouble, he taught me the principles of the nuggets. In those early years, I wasn't even sure of nugget #1. He didn't seem to be good at all when He let me struggle through months of unemployment and underemployment. But He had my best interests at heart even though I didn't enjoy His methods. He used that time to begin to teach me the lessons of the ash pit.

Let's go back a chapter or two and listen to Elihu again. This young man has a few things more to say. In the middle of his soliloquy, Elihu gives an explanation of the reasons behind God's exercise of His might. This one is pure gold. It helps me make sense out of the trouble that comes upon us.

> "Whether for correction, or for His world,
> Or for lovingkindness, He causes it to happen."
> (Job 37:13)

This verse speaks of three purposes that God might accomplish by allowing trouble in our lives. Number one is correction. If we are openly sinning and disobeying His word, He will allow trouble to overtake us in the form of the consequences of our actions. If we are stealing or harming others, He will allow us to be caught and suffer man's justice for a time. In my case, I was failing to acknowledge that God is my provider and my source of sustenance. He brought me low in this area so that I would acknowledge my need for Him. I didn't see this immediately, though. It took years for me to learn the lessons of the ash pit, and most cases it was only in hindsight. In some ways, I will never stop learning them.

The second purpose behind Trouble is a little more spiritual. Elihu says, "For His world." Sometimes He has a greater purpose in mind than we can fathom. He had a purpose for appearing in flesh and suffering on the cross in a world of Trouble. His purpose was greater than just bringing correction to one of His errant servants. It was to bring righteousness to the entire human race. Each of us has a part to play in this drama. We each receive the righteousness of Christ through faith in the cross, and we each are empowered to bring the righteousness of the cross to others. This is the mandate of the great commission: we are to preach the good news of how Jesus came through more trouble than any of us will ever experience. He came through the trouble of the cross to bring righteousness to all who would receive Him. This is His world, His purpose.

The third purpose here is lovingkindness. This is an old-fashioned word in English, so let's look at it in Hebrew.

The Hebrew word here that is translated as lovingkindness is the word *checed*. Here is how *Vine's Expository Dictionary of Biblical Words* defines *checed*.

> This word refers primarily to mutual and reciprocal rights and obligations between the parties of a relationship (especially Yahweh and Israel). But checed is not only a matter of obligation; it is also of generosity. It is not only a matter of loyalty, but also of mercy. The weaker party seeks the protection and blessing of the patron and protector, but he may not lay absolute claim to it. The stronger party remains committed to his promise, but retains his freedom, especially with regard to the manner in which he will implement those promises. Checed implies personal involvement and commitment in a relationship beyond the rule of law.[8]

This word is often translated as mercy, kindness, or goodness. It is a word that talks about the covenant relationship between the Lord and His people. Look at the last two sentences of the definition.

> The stronger party remains committed to his promise, but retains his freedom, especially with regard to the manner in which he will implement those promises. Checed implies personal involvement and commitment in a relationship beyond the rule of law

He is committed to fulfilling His promise of blessing upon His people, but He retains the right to fulfill that promise in whatever way He sees fit. Sometimes this means He may use methods that make us uncomfortable but that will ultimately work out for our good and for the good of others. It goes beyond fulfilling the letter of the promise of blessing to working all things in a manner which will achieve the ultimate good of blessing us, bringing correction to us and accomplishing His purpose in the world.

Yes, I was experiencing trouble as a way to bring correction to my errant soul, but in addition, He had a greater good in mind. He wanted to use the Trouble to accomplish a purpose in His kingdom. We'll get to that greater good later. But first He simply wanted me to repent of my arrogance and self-reliance.

In order to do this, He had to remove all the things in which I had put my confidence in myself, my job, my money, and my ability. Are you seeing a theme here? My, my, my. Thirty years ago, I didn't see it as clearly as I do now, but I knew that I needed to repent of my self-centered attitude. This was where Job found himself.

> "Therefore I retract,
> And I repent in dust and ashes." (Job 42:6)

When confronted with the greatness of God, I found myself on my face, repenting of my arrogance and selfishness. I acknowledged God and His provision in my life. Where Job was blameless, I was not—but I was forgiven. When I repented in brokenness, the Lord lifted me up from the ash pit and began to restore the things that the enemy had been allowed to steal.

It took years to do this, and throughout those years, I began to depend on God and His provision, acknowledging that any ability that I had was a gift from Him. He began to develop and cultivate other abilities in me that I had not even suspected were there. Yes, I was still able to use the abilities that I had before, but in addition, He added others that complemented the original abilities and enhanced my capacity to earn and provide. I now knew that what I had, I owed to Him, and I acknowledged that.

Why did I have to go through all this Trouble? Why did Job have to go through it? The answer is too simple. Through the Valley of Trouble is how we reach the greener pastures of peace and prosperity. There is no other way.

The Lord is my shepherd,
I shall not want.
He makes me lie down in green pastures;
He leads me beside quiet waters.
He restores my soul;
He guides me in the paths of righteousness
For His name's sake.
Even though I walk through the *valley of the shadow of death,*
I fear no evil, for You are with me;
Your rod and Your staff, they comfort me.
You prepare a table before me in the presence of my enemies;
You have anointed my head with oil;
My cup overflows.
Surely goodness and lovingkindness will
follow me all the days of my life,

And I will dwell in the house of the Lord forever.
(Ps. 23:1–6 my emphasis)

This most famous psalm begins with the peace of green pastures and still waters, and it ends in the house of the Lord. But right in the middle is the valley of the shadow of death. The phrase the translators chose here is the shadow of death, but the Hebrew word can mean ruin or destruction also. Nowhere in this verse does it say that the valley of the shadow of death is good or nice, but while we are passing through this not-so-nice place, we receive comfort from the Lord, our good shepherd. The comfort comes from His rod and staff. His rod and staff are symbols of His discipline and authority. With the rod, He deals out discipline to teach us what to do and what we should not do. With His staff, He gently guides us in the way we should go. He leads us through the valley to the green pastures, causes us to lie down in peace, and gives us good water to drink. He lavishly provides for our needs and prepares a covenant meal for us while our enemies rage outside. And best of all, when we are in this Valley of Trouble, He is right there beside us, delivering us from fear and walking us through the troubles. Jesus said it a differently, but the idea is still the same.

> "These things I have spoken to you, so that in Me you may have peace. In the world you have tribulation, but take courage; I have overcome the world." (John 16:33)

For someone who is in the valley, it would be easy to focus on the phrase "In the world you will have tribulation." But this must be taken in the context of the verse and in context with the previous chapters. He says, "These things I have spoken to you," meaning what He had been previously teaching. This lesson actually begins in the middle of chapter 13 of John's gospel. It is, in a way, His farewell address to His disciples. He has told them that He would be going away to prepare a place for them for all eternity. He has warned them that they would be persecuted for His sake, but that if they continued in His teaching, they would be fruitful in His kingdom. He has commanded them to continue in loving one another and Him. He has promised them the power and the comfort of the Holy Spirit, who He says will guide them into all truth. And He has told them that they would experience trouble, but these other things that He has told them would bring them peace in the midst of the trouble. He told them to take courage because He had overcome the world and all its trouble on their behalf.

What about Job, though? We left him in the ash pit sick, broke, childless, dejected, and on his face, repenting at the appearance of the Lord. God has appeared to him in the storm, and Job has found himself undone. He fears the power of the storm and sees himself unworthy in the face of a holy God, who has commanded the storm to appear and is speaking from within the storm. God is the God of the storm, over the storm and in the storm. When Job is in the middle of the trouble, God is there with him. When Job is in the storm, God still commands it and limits its ability to destroy. The disciples recognized this in the nature of Jesus. When He commanded the storm to be still, and it obeyed, they marveled, "What manner of man is this that the wind and waves obey?" (Mark 4:41). He demonstrated this nature to them so that all would know that He was the God of the storm, over the storm, and He was still God when He was in the middle of the storm with His disciples. He spoke to Job from the storm, He spoke to the storm in the middle of the lake, and He spoke to Job's friends from the middle of the storm.

> It came about after the Lord had spoken these words to Job, that the Lord said to Eliphaz the Temanite, "My wrath is kindled against you and against your two friends, because you have not spoken of Me what is right as My servant Job has. "Now therefore, take for yourselves seven bulls and seven rams, and go to My servant Job, and offer up a burnt offering for yourselves, and My servant Job will pray for you. For I will accept him so that I may not do with you according to your folly, because you have not spoken of Me what is right, as My servant Job has." So Eliphaz the Temanite and Bildad the Shuhite and Zophar the Naamathite went and did as the Lord told them; and the Lord accepted Job. (Job 42:7–9)

This is the beginning of the restoration process for Job. Job's friends have sinned by speaking things that were not true about the Lord. God wants to forgive them, and so He calls on His servant Job. Notice that Job is still called "My servant." In the storm, in the ash pit, and at the altar sacrificing on behalf of his friends, Job is still the servant of the Lord. His identity has not changed since the story began. In the Valley of Trouble, we too still belong to God. Job has a job to do here; it is not that different than what he was doing before the trouble. He is interceding and offering up sacrifices for others. Before, it was his children, and now it is his friends, but it is still the same. His office as priest and intercessor is being restored. Job is still covered with sores, and he's still brokenhearted, but he is to take his eyes off his own troubles and offer up a prayer for his three friends so that God might extend mercy to them despite their foolish speaking.

Job prayed for them, and the Lord accepted him. Some translations read "heard Job's prayer," but the literal translation of the Hebrew in this verse is more like "lifted up the face of Job." The Lord heard Job's prayer, lifted up Job's face toward Himself, and raised him up from the ash pit to stand before the altar of God.

This is what He does for us too. When we humble ourselves and bow before Him in true repentance, He raises us up from the ash pit of trouble to the throne room of heaven so that we can intercede for others and find restoration and healing, peace and freedom, and prosperity and grace to go forward with Him. It is only when we take our eyes off ourselves and our problems that we can be effective in His kingdom.

After Job prayed for his friends, the Lord began to restore the many blessings of his life.

> The Lord restored the fortunes of Job when he prayed for his friends, and the Lord increased all that Job had twofold. (Job 42:10)

Verse 10 tells us what God did. Verse 11 tells us how he started the process.

> Then all his brothers and all his sisters and all who had known him before came to him, and they ate bread with him in his house; and they consoled him and comforted him for all the adversities that the Lord had brought on him. And each one gave him one piece of money, and each a ring of gold. (Job 42: 11)

Notice that the Lord didn't restore Job's fortune all at once. He didn't win the lottery. Instead, his family gathered around him, comforted him, and shared with him what they had. Each of them gave him a piece of money. They didn't empty out their bank accounts. They simply shared what they had. Job took this money and put it to work, investing it over the next 140 years. Fourteen thousand sheep did not fall out of the sky into his sheep pens. Instead, Job humbly accepted the gifts that his friends and family brought to him, and he began again.

He began his family again too.

> He had seven sons and three daughters. (Job 42:13)

Now, you might ask, "Why does Job still have the same number of children—seven sons and three daughters? I thought he was supposed to get double." Actually, he had double the family because his first ten children were still living in heaven.

Therefore he had ten children with him and ten children waiting for him in heaven. God is faithful and true.

Yes, the Lord brought Job through the valley of the shadow of death, but He did not do it instantaneously. The text is clear: Job lived another 140 years. His children were not born all at once. To produce ten children must have taken several years. Job's flocks and herds did not suddenly manifest themselves in his pastures. He had to wait for his ewes to bear lambs and for his camels and cattle to calve. This did not happen overnight; it took years.

Our limited lifespan causes us humans to take a much shorter view of things than our eternal God takes. He is not governed by time, but because He placed us in a world that is governed by time, He chooses to work within the time frame of this world. Sometimes, however, He has his own idea about how to work within this time frame. He seems painfully slow to us, but He is really right on time. This is one of the most difficult things for us to understand and accept, but we must accept that He is the one who invented time, and so He must know what He is doing regarding the timing of His blessings.

This is another aspect of who He is that causes me, like Job, to clap my hand over my mouth in awe of a God who is eternal, standing outside of time but still willing to step into the time that He created to provide a savior for His creation. Jesus Himself became subject to time considerations when He entered the time frame which He created. Jesus recognized that He too, as a man, needed to wait until the time was right.

Now before the Feast of the Passover, Jesus
knowing that His hour had come that He would
depart out of this world to the Father, having
loved His own who were in the world, He loved
them to the end. (John 13:1)

He recognized that the timing was not even under His own
control, but under the authority of His Father.

He said to them, "It is not for you to know times
or epochs which the Father has fixed by His own
authority. (Acts 1:7–8)

This gives me a little encouragement on the timing thing. If
Jesus was subject to the Father's control regarding timing, then
I too can trust Him to bring about His purpose in His perfect
timing. Although this is encouraging, I still struggle with waiting
for God. It still doesn't make it pleasant to wait and wait, but Jesus
got through it, Job got through it, and I can too.

NUGGET #12

The Conclusion

The Lord blessed the latter days of Job more
than his beginning. (Job 42:12)

Yes, Job possessed more at the end of his life than he did at the beginning of the story, but that is not all there is to the story. The real blessing that Job received was not in the number of his livestock or even the beauty of his daughters. The real blessing of Job's life is still going on today.

A skeptic would look at the story of Job and say, "Why would a 'good' God put his favorite servant through such a time of torment? If God is truly good, then He would only do good things for his people, and they would then be happy, and He would be happy."

Those who say this are missing the point of the story. Yes, in a perfect world, this is how it would work. But we do not live in a perfect world. We live in a world that has been corrupted by sin and in which an enemy of our souls has engaged us in a spiritual battle for supremacy. The world in which we live contains much evil, and it must be overcome. How did this happen?

The omniscient God who created our world and declared it to be good gave our ancestor Adam authority over the earth.

> Then God blessed them, and God said to them, "Be fruitful and multiply; *fill the earth and subdue it; have dominion* over the fish of the sea, over the birds of the air, and over every living thing that moves on the earth." (Gen. 1:28 NKJV; my emphasis)

Adam took that authority which God had given and chose to disobey God. He gave himself over to the authority of the lying serpent and allowed that authority to bring a curse upon himself, his progeny, and the entire earth. Adam's disobedience is the source of Job's trouble because through it, the serpent (representing Satan) was given much authority over the earth. Job's story is the story of how God is redeeming the fallen world from the destruction unleashed by Adam's sin. God did not spare Job from the trouble; He brought him through the trouble.

As we read these words, we are encouraged by the way that Job was brought through his troubles. We can see that if the Lord brought Job through all his trials, then we too can survive and even thrive in the face of adversity. If we are looking for a reason behind the death and destruction that was visited upon Job, we need look no further than our own troubles.

Job's story became an encouragement to me when I was in the Valley of Trouble. His story encourages us all to believe that we can survive and even find meaning in our own struggles. Then as we overcome the troubles that come upon us, others are encouraged to persevere and keep fighting the good fight of faith. They are encouraged by our story and by the story of Job.

The longer that I spent in the valley, the more I got to know the heart of the Good Shepherd. I came to know the desire of the Master to bring good things to His people. I realized that He really had no desire to take away my things. Rather, He wanted me to learn to use the blessings and gifts that He had given me to bring glory to His name. In this way, I was able to find meaning in the struggle and to derive comfort from knowing that I was not alone. As I struggled, it was comforting to know that I was not the first to suffer loss, and I realized that I was never alone in the valley—my savior was right there with me every step of the way.

There was another way in which I was not alone in the valley. Like Job, I was going through the Valley of Trouble, but unlike Job, I had a helpmate who was not encouraging me to "curse God and die," but was encouraging me to pursue a closer relationship with my creator. Additionally, she was willing to step back out of the way and let God deal with me as He wanted.

The Proverbs say that a wife of noble character is worth more than rubies (Prov. 31:10). I don't know how Mrs. Job turned out past chapter 2, but I know that my own wife, Joy, was right there beside me throughout the whole process as I spent my time in the valley. My time in the valley was her time too. She felt the heat of the crucible, and she felt the pain of loss and disappointment, but she also knows the power of God's vindication. The testimony of her life is summed up in this verse: "Though He slay me, I will hope in Him"[9]

When things don't go right for her, she might moan and question God, saying, "Why?" But she never doubts that in the end, He will make things work out, even if she must wait for heaven to see things improve. She knows that her God has her best interests at heart, and she knows that He has saved her and will bring her to His courts to spend eternity with Him. She has always been amazingly consistent in this aspect of her character.

Her response to me today is the same response that she gave me years ago. Her response then was not, "Curse God and die." It was then and still is always, "Have you prayed about it? Have you asked God what you should do?"

Of course I hadn't asked Him about it. I was afraid to ask Him about it because then He might tell me that most of the trouble was of my own making. He might tell me what I should do about it, and then I would have to act on that knowledge. I would be responsible to do what He asked me to do. And what if He asked me to do something difficult or even impossible, or something that was outside my comfort zone?

I didn't want to ask because in my heart, I already knew the answer. I knew that I wasn't honoring God with my first fruits. I had grown up in a church that practiced New Testament Christianity. I had always been taught that tithing was an Old Testament, law of Moses thing. It was done away with by the cross. Yes, Christians were supposed to give and do so generously and cheerfully, but tithing was a thing of the past. We were supposed to give "as we had been prospered."[10] I was well aware of this scripture and didn't feel that I was "being prospered" at all. I felt no compunction to give even a little. Oh, I might drop a dollar or two into the collection on Sunday so it would look like I was contributing, but it was just for show, nothing else.

The congregation that we attended at that time did stress the importance of tithing and giving offerings above and beyond the tenth, but they had a different teaching on this subject than I had heard before. Their teaching was that the tithe was not because God needed it, but because tithing was the way that God's blessings would be released in the lives of the giver. The scriptural basis for this belief comes from the third chapter of the prophet Malachi.

> "Bring the whole tithe into the storehouse, so that there may be food in My house, and test Me now in this," says the Lord of hosts, "if I will not open for you the windows of heaven and pour out for you a blessing until it overflows. "Then I will rebuke the devourer for you, so that it will not destroy the fruits of the ground; nor will your vine in the field cast its grapes," says the Lord of hosts. "All the nations will call you blessed, for you shall be a delightful land," says the Lord of hosts. (Mal. 3:10–12 NASU)

The teaching was that God had no need of my money, but I had need of the blessing of God in my life. If I wanted to release the blessings of God, I needed to begin tithing. I know this teaching has been corrupted by some in the "prosperity gospel" movement, but the reality of scripture is not changed by men trying to misuse its principles to make themselves rich. The underlying principle is still valid. We need to return a portion of the blessings that God has bestowed on us—not for His sake, but for ours.

This was not the way that I had been taught, but I was in a desperate situation. I had to do something, anything. We were going down anyway, and so I reasoned, "Why not give this tithing thing a try?" We began tithing on what we had, my meager unemployment checks.

Now, I would like to say that everything turned around immediately, and we were suddenly and miraculously rolling in the dough, but that is not the way that it happened. It was gradual, over a period of months and years and decades. My employment situation began to change, and my attitude toward everything changed with it. I still had to deal with economic ups and downs and an industry that is inherently unstable, but I was beginning to put my faith in something—no, someone—other than myself and my abilities. Through lean times and fat, I learned to trust in my Lord's ability to supply my needs. Often it seemed that I learned more about this from the lean times than I did in the times of prosperity.

I have heard it said, "If you want to know where your heart is, look in the ledger of your checkbook." The places where you are spending your money and the places where you are giving your money are indicative of where your heart is. Where you spend what you have shows what is important to you and where your priorities lie.

If the me of those early years could have seen the ledger of my current checkbook, he would have been amazed and in disbelief. He would never have believed the amounts that now are there, the amounts that are going out, and to where those amounts are destined. I now look at giving as a way of investing in a kingdom that is eternal and that produces eternal rewards. Of course, I didn't see this back then when I started writing those checks. All I knew then was that something needed to change, and so I made the change that I could, taking baby steps of faith and gradually taking longer and longer strides. This is spiritual growth. It happens gradually, one day, one step, and one check at a time.

This is where Job is at the end of the book. His friends and relatives have come and given him some money to help him get back on his feet. How he invests that money is not specified in the text, but it is obvious that Job understands business, and he understands God's principles of giving because he turns this nest egg into a fortune twice the size of his original fortune.

The real blessing of the latter part of Job's life was not the fortune that he acquired in his later years. Neither is it the children who were born in his house. These are simply physical things which can be counted as blessings. The real blessing of Job's life is still going on today, however. The countless lives that Job's story has touched, including mine as I write and yours as you read these words, are the real legacy of Job's life and the simple explanation of why Job had to endure such hardship. The testimony of Job's life helps us to overcome the enemy, Satan, who falsely accused Job and does the same to us.

> "And they overcame him [Satan] because of the
> blood of the Lamb and *because of the word of their*

testimony, and they did not love their life even when faced with death." (Rev. 12:11)

In a sense, Job is still overcoming the enemy today with the word of his testimony. Every time someone reads the words of Job's story and is encouraged to trust in the Lord, to step out in faith, or to not give up, Job's testimony is overcoming the accuser again. This is the true blessing of the later part of Job's life: the countless lives that he has touched by his story over more than three thousand years. His is a life of gold taken through the ash pit and raised up to the pinnacle of heaven to stand before the face of God.

Job's story is a constant blessing to me, and it will be to you too. It encourages me to look up and remember that God is ultimately good, and even if He allows circumstances to bring trouble into my life, He has a plan to use it to bring about an ultimate good.

Is everything perfect all the time? Of course not! I don't think everything was perfect for Job either. Happily ever after is a fairy tale. Job lived in, and we live in the real world. I'm sure that when Job's ten children became teenagers, he had his doubts about whether they were a blessing at all. Sometimes his livestock got sick, and sometimes his hired men stole from him. These are simply circumstances. They are not a blessing or a curse. They are part of the fallen world in which we live, and they will continue to be so until God finishes the process of bringing redemption to this world.

If, like Job, we can stand in the midst of the ashes and declare, "Even though He slay me, yet will I trust Him," then we are a part of Job's legacy. We have the ability to pass that legacy along to others who are experiencing the ash pit.

Those of us who have been touched by Job's story and have received comfort from it can stand right beside him and offer up praises to God. Like Job, we are nuggets of gold that have endured the heat of the crucible and have come out refined, purified, and suitable for the master's service. I am one of the legacies of Job's life, and you, dear reader, can be too. All of us who can learn from Job's time in the ash pit are the true nuggets of gold that God has recovered from the ash pit of life. He rejoices as He gently holds us in the crucible of His hands and shapes us into the precious treasure that He desires. You, dear reader, are a nugget of gold, and your savior rejoices over you.

APPENDIX

I have bad news, and I have good news. The bad news comes first. If you are not a Christian, then you are a sinner. These are the only two choices. Simply put, sinners are people who commit sin.

We all know what sin is. It is disobedience to God's laws: stealing, lying, murdering, hating, doing something that is wrong or evil. The Bible tells us that "all have sinned and come short of the glory of God."[B] We were once all in this same boat. I was there, my pastor was there, and even the person who gave you this book was there. We all are born with a sin nature that we inherited from our ancestor Adam, the first sinner.

If you are a sinner who has done anything that you shouldn't, then you are condemned by your own sin to die and spend an eternity of torment in a place called Hell.[C] I can't imagine how long eternity is but I know that I don't want to spend a minute in Hell.

The worse news is that there is nothing that you can do on your own to remedy this situation. I know this sounds bad, but stick with me.

[B] Romans 3:23.
[C] Romans 6:23.

Here comes the good news. It doesn't have to stay that way. There is nothing that any of us can do that would save us from this eternal fate, but God in His mercy has provided us with a way to escape this terrible fate.[D] His name is Jesus, and He is God's firstborn son. This divine Son became one of His creations and lived as a man two thousand years ago in the Middle East. He lived a sinless life, loving and caring for the people around Him and challenging the status quo. He was crucified as a criminal even though He had done nothing wrong, and as He hung upon the cross, along with Him hung all the sins of the entire world. This sinless Son took upon Himself all of my sin, your sin, and everyone else's sin. He endured the punishment that we rightly deserved so that justice would be done. He took the punishment that was due us so we wouldn't have to. Then He went to this place called hell and took away the keys from the devil who rules there. This is how much He loves us.

To prove that Jesus had triumphed over sin and death, God raised His Son from the tomb on the first day of the week.[E] This is the source of our hope. Because Jesus was resurrected from the grave, so shall we who believe in Him be resurrected and receive eternal life. This promise of salvation from sin and eternal life is available to all who will call upon the name of the Lord.[F] How, then, do we call on the name of the Lord? It is really as simple as following these steps.

[D] Romans 5:6.

[E] Romans 6:4–9.

[F] Romans 10:9–10, 13.

Acknowledge that you are a sinner in need of salvation.

Repent of this sin and ask for forgiveness. To repent means to turn back or away from something. Jesus is ready to forgive any who will ask. He went to the cross just for this.

Publicly recognize Jesus as the Son of the Living God and your Lord and master who died for your sins and rose again to new life so that you too can have eternal life. (By public, I mean out loud, not just silently to yourself. I don't necessarily mean on the street corner, but if that's how you feel, more power to you. A good place to do this would be with a friend who you know is a Christian.)

If you can take those steps and really mean it from your heart, that is all it takes to become a Christian. The real adventure starts now. Your master has a plan for you, blessings to give you, work for you to do in His kingdom, and a place for you at His table. The best part of this is that you are not alone in this. He will be right there by your side to help you, encourage you, and sometimes even carry you through. In addition, He will bring other believers like you alongside you to help keep you on the right path, to lift you up when you stumble, and to celebrate with you when you triumph. This is the beauty of Christianity: we are not in this alone. Christ is right here with us all the time, and so are His people.

A good place for you to start is with the person who gave you this book. Chances are he or she is not the first to try to lead you down this road, and it probably is not the first attempt. Go to him, tell him how you asked Jesus to forgive you and received Him as Lord and savior, and ask him to show you the next steps in your new life. He will be excited and thrilled. It is likely something that he has been praying for himself. He can also direct you to a Bible-believing church that is filled with others who will help you along the way.

The local church can help to lead you into the steps of baptism and communion. The church is a community of believers united in purpose of fulfilling the will of Christ. Now you, as a believer, are part of that community, and you have a part to play in it.

Also, get out your own Bible and look up the references in the footnotes of this appendix. Read the verses not just by themselves but in their context. The Bible is like a lifeline attaching you to the Savior. Hold on tight to it and keep it with you, referring to it as you read the rest of this book. My greatest desire for this book is that it will inspire others to find strength and joy in the written word of God.

ENDNOTES

1   We don't hear any more from Job's wife after this. I don't know if he made her angry and she left, or if she saw the wisdom in his words and let him be alone in his grief. Later, she was reconciled to God, we hope, and had ten more children to replace the ten she'd lost.

An early Jewish tradition holds that Job's wife was Dinah, the daughter of Jacob, who was raped by the prince of Shechem and the subject of her brothers' vengeance on the Shechemites (Gen. 34). If this tradition represents the truth, Dinah (if she was Job's wife) was well acquainted with trouble and was raised by a father who recognized the Lord.

2   Most Bible scholars place Job in the Patriarchal period, which is roughly from Noah to Moses. Although there is some doubt as to the exact timing of Job's life, it is clear that he is in a period that is prior to the giving of the Torah on the Mountain because the book makes no reference at all to the Law. On the other end, the names of Job's friends indicate that they lived later than Abraham. Eliaphaz is a Temanite hailing from a town in Edom, which bears the name of one of Esau's sons, or possibly even being descended from Esau's son Teman. This would place him later than Abraham by at least several decades, and maybe centuries. Elihu is described as the son of a Buzite, who would be a descendant of Buz, the son of Nahor, Abraham's younger brother. This clearly places two of the friends in the post-Abrahamic period but before the Exodus, likely during the 430-year period of Israelite slavery.

3   The writer of the epistle to the Hebrews described Judaism as a shadow of heavenly things (Heb. 10:1, 8:5) and Paul described observance of the Torah as shadow of the things to come (Col. 2: 17). According to Paul, the substance, the thing which produces or casts the shadow, is Jesus.

4   Holy Bible, New Living Translation, copyright ©1996, 2004 by Tyndale Charitable Trust. Used by permission of Tyndale House Publishers. All rights reserved.

5   In Deut. 19:6 the redeemer is called the "avenger of blood," whose duty it was to execute the murderer of his relative. From *Vine's Expository Dictionary of Biblical Words* (Thomas Nelson Publishers, 1985).

     In this instance, Job is referring to Jesus's triumphant return to earth to deal Satan his final defeat, avenging all the wrongs done to God's people.

6   Rick Renner, *Sparkling Gems from the Greek* (Teach All Nations, 2003).

7   Over the years, I have done this program several times and have never failed to be blessed. I highly recommend it to anyone who truly wants to grow in relationship with the Lord. For those who have a smart phone, the Bible apps that we use often include reading programs like this, which make it simple to keep up.

8   *Vine's Expository Dictionary of Biblical Words* (Thomas Nelson Publishers, 1985).

9   Job 13:15a (NASU).

10   1 Cor. 16:2.

ABOUT THE AUTHOR

Michael Howard is a retired Ironworker and lifelong student of the Bible who has spent nearly twenty years as a lay Bible study leader and teacher. His unique insights into the Bible are inspiring and encouraging to believers and non-believers alike. He has a 'blue collar' approach to the bible and uses this to draw non-scholars into deeper study of God's word.